"Research indicates that young adults today hope to have success-ful, long-term marriages, but for many reasons they are not sure that such relationships are possible. The Rodgers' get to the root of these concerns and provide hope and encouragement for those singles who seek to develop healthy and loving relationships on the pathway toward marriage."

—DENNIS LOWE, PhD, director,
Center for the Family, Pepperdine University

"Drs. Tom and Beverly Rodgers have written an authentic, empower-ing guide for singles that addresses the many reasons individuals are hesitant to marry. It includes a bevy of suggestions, Scriptures, and resources to encourage and uplift during the inevitable soul-searching this book will bring about."

—ERIC AND JENNIFER GARCIA, cofounders,
Association of Marriage and Family Ministries

"Drs. Tom and Beverly Rodgers have left no stone unturned in researching *The Singlehood Phenomenon*. Their findings and real case studies throughout the book should encourage skeptical singles to confront their fears and misgivings about marriage and to believe that love and marriage can become a realized dream."

—FREDA V. CREWS, DMin, PhD,
TV host and university dean

"*The Singlehood Phenomenon* is a phenomenon in and of itself. The way in which Drs. Tom and Bev Rodgers candidly address the reasons why singles are opting out of getting married is both informative and refreshing. It is imperative to know where singles stand if we are to offer them anything that will take them beyond the mundane and into an understanding of marriage that exceeds the norm."

—PHIL WAUGH, executive director,
Covenant Marriage Movement

"Today's singles grew up learning more about how relationships end than how they can be sustained. Drs. Beverly and Tom Rodgers offer life-changing insight and helpful instruction for those who find them-selves unintentionally single."

—JEN ABBAS, author of *Generation Ex: Adult Children of Divorce and the Healing of Our Pain*

The Singlehood
Phenomenon

10 Brutally Honest Reasons
People Aren't Getting Married

Beverly Rodgers PhD and Tom Rodgers PhD

NAVPRESS®

BRINGING TRUTH TO LIFE

OUR GUARANTEE TO YOU

The Navigators is an international Christian organization. Our mission is to advance the gospel of Jesus and His kingdom into the nations through spiritual generations of laborers living and discipling among the lost. We see a vital movement of the gospel, fueled by prevailing prayer, flowing freely through relational networks and out into the nations where workers for the kingdom are next door to everywhere.

NavPress is the publishing ministry of The Navigators. The mission of NavPress is to reach, disciple, and equip people to know Christ and make Him known by publishing life-related materials that are biblically rooted and culturally relevant. Our vision is to stimulate spiritual transformation through every product we publish.

© 2006 by Beverly and Thomas Alan Rodgers

All rights reserved. No part of this publication may be reproduced in any form without written permission from NavPress, P.O. Box 35001, Colorado Springs, CO 80935.
www.navpress.com

NAVPRESS, BRINGING TRUTH TO LIFE, and the NAVPRESS logo are registered trademarks of NavPress. Absence of ® in connection with marks of NavPress or other parties does not indicate an absence of registration of those marks.

ISBN 1-57683-884-6

Cover design by Cover Story Book Design Group / Brannon McAllister and Dailey Crafton
Cover photo by Getzcreative Photography
Creative Team: Terry Behimer, Andrea Christian, Cara Iverson, Reagen Reed, Arvid Wallen, Kathy Guist

Some of the anecdotal illustrations in this book are true to life and are included with the permission of the persons involved. All other illustrations are composites of real situations, and any resemblance to people living or dead is coincidental.

Unless otherwise identified, all Scripture quotations in this publication are taken from the *New King James Version* (NKJV). Copyright © 1982 by Thomas Nelson, Inc. Used by permission. All rights reserved. Other versions used include: the HOLY BIBLE: NEW INTERNATIONAL VERSION® (NIV®), Copyright © 1973, 1978, 1984 by International Bible Society, used by permission of Zondervan Publishing House, all rights reserved; *THE MESSAGE* (MSG). Copyright © 1993, 1994, 1995, 1996, 2000, 2001, 2002. Used by permission of NavPress Publishing Group; and *The Living Bible* (TLB), copyright © 1971, used by permission of Tyndale House Publishers, Inc., Wheaton, IL 60189, all rights reserved.

Rodgers, Beverly, 1954-
  The singlehood phenomenon : 10 brutally honest reasons people
aren't getting married / Beverly Rodgers and Tom Rodgers.
    p. cm.
  Includes bibliographical references.
  ISBN 1-57683-884-6
  1. Marriage--United States--Psychological aspects. 2. Single men
--United States--Psychology. 3. Single women--United States
--Psychology. 4. Man-woman relationships--United States
--Psychological aspects. I. Rodgers, Tom, 1950- . II. Title.
HQ536.R62 2006
248.8'4--dc22

2006018409

Printed in the United States of America

1 2 3 4 5 6 / 10 09 08 07 06

FOR A FREE CATALOG OF NAVPRESS BOOKS & BIBLE STUDIES,
CALL 1-800-366-7788 (USA) OR 1-800-839-4769 (CANADA).

Contents

Acknowledgments

This book could not have been written without the openness and honesty of the singles who have participated in our focus groups across the country. We want to express gratitude to them and to those who have sat across from us in the counseling office for the last twenty-six years and trusted us with their deep heart's desire to get married, even at a time in our culture when marriage was not in vogue. You have honored us with your vulnerability and courage in your search for your soul's mate. We also applaud those of you who have journeyed with us by reading this material.

We want to thank our own searching single daughters, Amanda, 25, and Nicole, 23, for your honest input and patience as we worked long and hard hours putting this book together.

Finally, we want to thank NavPress for publishing this material, and our editors—Andrea Christian, Reagen Reed, and Cara Iverson—for fine-tuning this manuscript and inspiring us with your tireless energy.

Introduction

The marriage rate in the United States has dropped drastically in the last decade. As a result, we have the oldest and largest singles population in our nation's history. This has created concern both among social scientists who feel that marriage is the foundation of culture and society and among theologians who believe that marriage is the earthly replication of the spiritual relationship between humanity and God.

That being said, we don't believe there is anything wrong with being single. Some people stay single because they do not feel like they need a partner to be fulfilled. This is a healthy move, and we support singles who are content. However, there are many people who desire to be married, but are reticent because of fears and concerns that stand in their way and the stigma about marriage that permeates our society.

Traditional marriage is under attack—to such an extent that many singles question the relevance of matrimony. Many social scientists now believe that the weakening of marriage is a genuine social crisis. Michael Craven of the National Coalition for the Protection of Children and Families says, "Across America the institution of marriage is being assailed, reduced to nothing more than a sentimental ceremony between consenting adults, radically redefined, or simply abandoned altogether."[1]

Unfortunately, there are valid reasons for society to be down on marriage. The high divorce rate in our country is perhaps one of the main ones. Some statistics show that in the last decade the nation's divorce rate hit 56 percent before it pulled back. It now hovers around 50 percent. One in two marriages ends, and this statistic does not include those who are unhappy and feel trapped in their marriages. Everyone seems to know a couple with marital trouble. Today's singles wonder if marriage is all it is cracked up to be and are turning instead to alternatives such as cohabitation, nonmarried coparenting, and common-law marriage.

Many singles have pushed dating way down on their list of priorities. Some have grown cynical; others have given up all together. If you are one of these singles, this book is for you. The information contained in these pages will help you uncover unconscious beliefs, unhealthy behaviors, and toxic relationship patterns that could be sabotaging your love life. We also address the growing *singlehood phenomenon* in our culture and the top ten reasons why singles aren't getting married. But don't despair! We'll give you practical and biblical ways to overcome these reasons. If you are working with singles as a pastor, mentor, or counselor, this book will be a valuable resource as you guide singles to establish healthy relationships and challenge them to see marriage, as well as singlehood, in a more positive light.

My husband, Tom, and I have been married for twenty-nine years and Christian relationship counselors for twenty-six years. We have helped hundreds—if not thousands—of singles, couples, and families learn to develop healthy, lasting, and godly relationships. The work we've done in our own marriage and the insight we've gained from counseling led to the development of a model of relationships called the *Soul Healing Love Model*. Tom and I never set out to develop a model; we simply wanted to heal our own wounded marriage. Our personal and professional experience has taught us that we all suffer from emotional and

physical pain that affects our ability to have healthy relationships. We have dedicated ourselves to determining what makes
relationships work and what causes them to fail. Our search for
answers and for healing led to what we consider the culmina-
tion of our life's work.

The Soul Healing Love Model integrates biblical and
psychological principles to help people deal with the wounds
they have received in life, particularly in childhood. The Soul
Healing Love Model will give you practical tools and techniques designed to bring about awareness and insight, enhance
empathy, and foster forgiveness so that you can be the healthiest person possible. Healing your soul wounds will allow you to
break free from unhealthy and sometimes unconscious patterns,
which may be hindering your ability to have healthy relationships. Most importantly, we'll show you how God's unconditional love can heal your woundedness so that you become a
healing agent to those around you and, eventually, your spouse.

The Soul Healing Love Model has helped countless singles
find true and lasting love. It is not easy; it involves a soul searching that you may find uncomfortable and even, at times, painful. We'll challenge you to look at past hurts and determine
how they have affected you as an adult, particularly in intimate
relationships. We've found that singles who take this journey
develop a renewed faith in love, marriage, their future, and even
God. Some have made peace with their current stage in life;
others have found their soul mates. Throughout this book, you'll
find stories of these successful singles. We hope you will get to
know them, relate to them, and that their stories will encourage
and inspire you.

As you read the pages of this book, you will see that it is
written from my (Bev's) perspective. However, Tom was a part
of the manuscript every step of the way. You will often read
the words *we*, *our*, or *us*. This is because we are a team, both in

marriage and in ministry. The concepts in this book are a result of years of conversations, lecture preparations, books, articles, and case studies.

Our prayer for you is that you will learn to be the healthiest, happiest single person you can be, but also that you will learn, with God's help, to overcome your fear of marriage and the reasons that keep you single.

Skepticism About Love and Marriage

I'd rather be alone than in a bad marriage

Lisa was an attractive, athletic, twenty-six-year-old paralegal who attended law school at a very prestigious university. She was pretty, stayed in shape, and had plenty of friends. Lisa truly lived the good life in her uptown condo with her loyal Labrador retriever, Buddy. Lisa attended church regularly, participated in an accountability group, and went to a singles Bible study every week. She seemed to have everything going for her, but despite her success and a perpetual flurry of activity, she was frustrated and lonely. Her life was filled with friends, school, church, and family, but something was missing. Lisa wanted a companion, someone to walk beside her through life's struggles.

Lisa came to counseling after hearing us speak on a local radio station about why singles are afraid to marry. At first, she was skeptical about marriage and wouldn't even acknowledge that she wanted a husband. We found that Lisa did not let herself want a husband because she couldn't take the disappointment and pain of not getting one. It was easier for her to indulge in skepticism about the institution of marriage.

THE GROWING SINGLES POPULATION

Lisa's story is all too common these days. The growth of the singles population supports that she is not alone in feeling down on love and marriage. According to the United States Census Bureau, the number of singles has more than quadrupled in the last thirty years. In 1970 there were only 21.4 million singles, which constituted only 10 percent of the population. In the 2004 population study, that figure rose to a staggering 88 million (42 million men and 46 million women),[1] equaling 31 percent of the population. As the singles population grows older and larger, skepticism about love increases. People like Lisa are not just ever-increasing numbers on a demographics chart—they are real people who desire a healthy marriage but do not know how to achieve their goal. We can empathize with the nation's singles because there are so many valid reasons for their skepticism.

REASONS FOR SKEPTICISM

Fear of Making a Mistake. Almost everyone knows a couple in a difficult or even miserable marriage. Today's singles are afraid that they will pick the wrong mate. We often hear, "I'd rather be alone than in a bad marriage."

The High Divorce Rate. Marriage has stopped being "for keeps." Singles do not want to be trapped in a bad marriage, but they do not want to divorce either. Half of Generation X (those born between 1965 and 1978) suffered through the divorce of their parents, and adult children of divorced couples are often afraid to get married because they do not want to go through the pain their parents suffered. They're also aware of statistics showing that children of divorce have a higher divorce rate in their own marriages.

Relational Insecurity. Children of divorce often feel

inadequate and somewhat handicapped when it comes to establishing intimacy, because they do not have role models to teach them. Tom and I call this *relational insecurity*. Jen Abbas, in her book *Generation Ex: Adult Children of Divorce and the Healing of Our Pain*, speaks of this when she writes,

> Even though I was successful academically and professionally, I found myself becoming more insecure each year about my emotional abilities. As I began to see my friends marry, I started to question my ability to successfully create and maintain intimate relationships, especially my own future marriage.... I was paralyzed because what I wanted so desperately was that which I feared the most.[2]

Those whose parents are still married also feel inadequate when it comes to making marriage work. The changing roles of men and women have caused traditional marriages to seem obsolete, and without a blueprint, singles feel as though they are floundering. To avoid feeling inadequate or insecure, they often focus on the areas of their lives where they feel more capable of succeeding, such as work, church, education, or physical fitness.

Fear of Getting Hurt. Love relationships can be painful. Many singles have been wounded and now equate dating and mating with hurt and pain. Their fear of getting hurt causes them to stop looking for a soul mate. Some have stopped believing in a soul mate and think the concept was developed by the media to promote "chick flicks" and romance novels.

The Narcissistic Culture. The "me" mentality of our culture has fed the psyches of many singles who believe marriage will force them to give up their personal freedom. Many see marriage as confinement and constraint, rather than an opportunity for connection and belonging.

Consumerism. Singles in our focus groups tell us that some of their skepticism about marriage is related to the societal trend toward consumerism. Our culture tells you that with the click of a button, you can get anything you want, in any color, shape, or size. To quote one man in a focus group, "Just look at the supermarkets today. There are a million choices in foods, hygiene products, and soapsuds. I have trouble choosing toothpaste. How can I possibly choose the right mate?"

Fear of Acrimonious Disputes. Singles fear that marriage will lead to emotional suffering and social shame. Divorce settlements are often hostile and very public, causing singles to turn away from their God-given desire to marry.

THE DISAPPEARANCE OF MATRIMONY

Because of the reasons listed above, matrimony is disappearing in our culture. Much of the contemporary sociological research of our day focuses on the growing trend of singleness in our nation. At Rutgers University, the National Marriage Project dedicated an entire issue of its *2002 The State of Our Unions Report* to the study of why so many men are not getting married.[3] The Centers for Disease Control's July 2002 report featured statistics on the current trends in marriage and cohabitation, which showed that the marriage rate is dropping.[4] In 2004, *The State of Our Unions Report* studied patterns of single men in order to determine "who's the marrying kind" and found that men are marrying later, if at all.[5] A *Time* magazine cover showed a single mom with her son and a caption reading, "The New American Family." The article explored the growing cultural trend of single-parent families. Even our government has become concerned that the nation is giving up on the idea of matrimony and has allocated federal monies to promote marriage.

SINGLES ARE GIVING UP

Because of their skepticism about marriage, many singles like Lisa tell us that they have stopped going to singles groups. They don't date. Some don't even socialize with members of the opposite sex. They go to work and attend church, then go home and watch television.

Because she did not date, Lisa started to believe that there was something wrong with her. She asked us, "Why am I still single? I always meet every goal that I set, but I am really afraid that I can't meet this one. I can't help thinking that something must be wrong with me."

Singles like Lisa often feel rejected, unacceptable, or unworthy as they grow older. This feeling causes them to become critical of themselves. Lisa blamed herself for being single and focused on all of her shortcomings. Her self-talk was extremely self-deprecating, and as her confidence waned, she gave up on dating.

Giving up on dating and mating only reinforces feelings of unworthiness. Singles who find themselves discouraged or hopeless need to seek the Lord and prayerfully ask Him to guide them as they do a healthy soul-searching and self-evaluation. An honest, God-inspired look inside should bring about insight and understanding. It should never result in self-blame and self-deprecation. We have a maxim in the Soul Healing Love Model that states, "In order to find a healthy soul mate, you must first find the healthy soul mate within you." As you read through the pages of this book, we will help you facilitate such introspection.

FEAR OF WANTING

We challenged Lisa to look inward and she found that there might indeed be internal reasons why she was still single. Lisa saw that not only was she afraid to want a husband, she was also afraid to tell anyone in her circle of single friends about her heart's desire for a mate. She was scared to share her feelings because she did not want to appear desperate or needy. "It's like this unwritten rule in our group that you should not show that you want a mate," Lisa confessed. "If you do, others will think you are unfulfilled or weak. I feel guilty for wanting a man in my life—like I'm not independent or self-sufficient enough."

Our society's emphasis on independence can make you feel weak for wanting a mate and leave you with the expectation that you should be happy with your autonomy.

Most of the material on singleness in the Christian world focuses on being content. Supporters of this belief quote Philippians 4:11, "I have learned in whatever state I am, to be content." If singles are not content, they often feel like bad Christians. Of course, you should strive to be content as a single person, but this does not mean that you should hide your God-given desire for a mate under a facade of self-sufficiency.

REACTION FORMATION

In psychological terms, concealing or minimizing a deep (and very normal) longing is known as *reaction formation*. Sigmund Freud, the father of psychoanalysis, coined the term to describe a defense mechanism in humans in which we do and say the *opposite* of what we are feeling in order to hide our true desires. His classic example was the temperance worker in the early 1920s who secretly imbibed liquor in the closet. A desire for alcohol was masked by an overt and rather vehement protest against it.

Many singles use the defense of reaction formation to conceal their hidden longing for a mate. Writer Christina Nehring saw evidence of this while reviewing the plethora of singles books available today. In the January 2002 issue of *Atlantic Monthly* she writes,

> While many singles report that they try to hide their interest in this genre, these books draw astonishing numbers of readers. Many of these doubtless consider themselves ironic or atypical; but ironic audiences are often the most faithful of all. In fact, the assumption in literature is not pleasure seeking but desperate; not confident, adventuresome, and looking for tips on how to have a good time, but frightened and looking for hints on how to avoid disaster.[6]

WANTING A MATE IS NORMAL

These "ironic or atypical" singles should not have to hide what is normal. Our culture tries hard to portray contentment and independence as the main goals of the single life, but the desire for a mate is God-given. In Genesis 2, the creation story, the only thing God declared "not good" was that man was alone. The first man, Adam, saw that he was alone and wanted companionship and intimacy. Because of his need, God fashioned a helper suitable for him. Adam was hardwired for love; in fact, all humans are.

Rose Sweet, in her book *Dear God, Send Me a Soul Mate*, shares the story of Eliezer, Abraham's servant, who was given the daunting task of finding Abraham's son Isaac a mate. Eliezer took his job seriously and prayed that God would guide his every move. The hand of God guided Eliezer and he finally found the beautiful, caring Rebecca, who was the perfect partner for Isaac. Sweet writes,

> From the beginning of time, God has called us to Himself. Our deepest desires for intimacy, love and belonging, our

desire for a soul mate, come from Him, and ultimately they are for Him. God does not always give you what you want. He does give you everything you would want if you could see what He sees and know what He knows. Don't deny your desire for a soul mate, and don't demand that God provide one for you immediately. Instead, share it with your Heavenly Father and ask for His special blessings. Put your hand in His, and let Him teach you wonderful things.[7]

LISA'S HEALING

God had many things to teach Lisa as she started to deal with her skepticism about marriage and acknowledge her desire for a soul mate. Lisa saw that one of the biggest reasons she was skeptical about love was that she did not think that she (or anyone, for that matter) could do the hard work to make it last. "Why can't it be easier?" she lamented. "Why do love and marriage have to be so hard?" We shared with Lisa that "happily-ever-after" often takes conscious, arduous effort. You cannot take two different people from two different families and merge them together without work. However, God would use this challenge to help her and her future husband become the people He wanted them to be.

THE "US" OF MARRIAGE

We believe that each person has a divine destiny or call, but a couple has a divine destiny as well. Marriage is a hallowed crucible where couples grow together into oneness and establish the divine "us." This is the combination of two people who together, with God's help, find the purpose for which they were created.

Tom and I have found our "us" and developed it for the past thirty years. We know that what we are able to accomplish as a couple is greater than what we could have accomplished on our own. Finding our purpose as a couple has been one of the most rewarding things we have done in our lives.

LISA'S HAPPY ENDING

Eventually, Lisa was ready to take the next step in her journey. Fueled with a lot of faith, she started going to a large singles group in her area where she made several friends, both male and female. They invited her to attend the social functions they sponsored: cookouts at the lake and evening baseball games. Some of the group members were planning a square dance at their church and Lisa volunteered to help publicize the event. The group had given so much to her that she wanted to give something back.

Lisa received a call from Scott, a reporter for a local neighborhood newspaper who wanted to do a story about the dance. She met him for coffee and excitedly told him about the group and the events they were planning. Assuming Scott was married, she was totally herself in the interview. Lisa was never nervous around married guys, but if they were single, good-looking, and available she often got tongue-tied. He was obviously relaxed with her too, because he asked her out right on the spot! It was not until that moment that she realized he was single. Lisa accepted the date, which at one point would have been out of her comfort zone.

Lisa and Scott started the process of getting to know each other, and a great friendship began to bloom. As time passed, their friendship turned into romance. They came to several sessions of relationship counseling and attended a Soul Healers Couples Weekend, a fifteen-hour intensive workshop where couples learn how their past has affected them and how to build a healthy, godly relationship.

Lisa and Scott have been married for two years and they've discovered that part of their purpose as a couple is to do missions work. They've taken many trips to South America and plan to adopt a child from there and start a family. Lisa is overflowing with happiness that she was able to overcome her skepticism about love and marriage and, in the process, found that God is indeed faithful.

MAKING IT PRACTICAL: WHAT ABOUT ME?

At the end of each chapter are questions for reflection and beliefs from Scripture that will help you to interact with the material. You can use this section for personal reflection or group study. Take a few minutes, get in a quiet place, and prayerfully and honestly answer the questions. You may want to keep a separate journal to record your thoughts, insights, and prayer requests.

What about you? If God is telling you that He wants to help you overcome your fear or distrust of marriage, read on. There is hope. Just wait and see.

FOR FURTHER THOUGHT

1. Did reading this chapter uncover any skepticism you feel about marriage? Which of the reasons for skepticism do you most relate to?

2. Sometimes acknowledging a need that is unmet can be painful. Have you, like Lisa, ever used the defense of reaction formation to conceal your longing for a spouse?

3. Often, we're so focused on society's negative view of marriage that we forget marriage is intended to help us become who God has called us to be. Is there a couple you know whose marriage you admire? What do you observe about their purpose as a couple?

GROWING YOUR FAITH

- Humans are hardwired for love. My desire for a mate is normal and I do not have to hide it.

     And the LORD God said, "It is not good that man should be alone; I will make him a helper comparable to him." (Genesis 2:18)

- God is in control of my future and will guide me as I select a mate.

     "For I know the plans that I have for you," says the LORD. "They are plans for good and not for evil, to give you a future and a hope." (Jeremiah 29:11, TLB)

- I can surrender my skepticism about love and marriage to God because He is trustworthy.

     "In those days when you pray, I will listen. You will find me when you seek me, if you look for me in earnest." (Jeremiah 29:12-13, TLB)

Lack of Faith in God's Provision

I'm not sure if I have a soul mate

Annie was a thirty-two-year-old surgical resident who made it through medical school in record time. She came into our counseling office because she was losing hope that she would ever get married. Annie had had several short-lived relationships and each breakup caused her faith to wane a little bit more. After each relationship ended, she would bury herself in work. Because of her skill and compassion, Annie was a successful and sought-after physician, but she felt there was more to life. She told us, "I love my work and feel I am fulfilling the purpose that God has put me here for, but I always thought that He had a husband for me as well. I never thought that I would spend my life alone."

When we asked Annie about her social life, she told us she didn't really have one. She had given up on meeting men. In fact, she had such a negative opinion of them that she had sworn off dating altogether. Most of her time and energy was spent at the hospital caring for patients. She would go in evenings and weekends, even when she wasn't on call, just to make sure they were all right.

Annie felt pretty hopeless about finding a soul mate and was considering adopting a child so that she could at least experience motherhood. Sadly, she had even stopped praying for a soul mate because she felt the Lord had abandoned her. She stopped going to church, and though she blamed this mostly on her heavy work schedule, the truth was, she felt that the Lord had let her down. She was mad at men for rejecting her. She was mad at God because He had not fulfilled her heart's desire according to her timeline.

Annie dealt with her losses by talking herself out of her need for love. She told herself she did not need a man. In her mind, there were no good men out there anyway. Besides, she had several friends who were struggling in their marriages, so perhaps marriage wasn't all that great. As a result, Annie retreated into solitude and tried to count the blessings of being single.

At first she justified her feelings by saying that she was following Paul's instructions in 1 Corinthians 7:8-9 when he says, "But I say to the unmarried and to the widows: It is good for them if they remain [single] even as I am." Annie told herself she was emulating Paul so that she could serve the Lord, but deep inside she was disillusioned and hurt. We helped her understand that Paul did not say there is anything wrong with marriage. Paul felt that it was better to perform Christian service as a single person so that you are able to devote more of your time to the work of God's kingdom. However, he did not say that being single is the only way to serve the Lord.

It may be easy for you as a single person to use Paul's passage to mask your true desire for a soul mate. You may hide behind your work, Christian service, or ministry because you fear being disappointed in love. Like Annie, you may be afraid to want marriage because you don't want to be disappointed. Annie reported that even though there were benefits to being single, "counting her blessings" was getting old. It no longer helped her deal with disappointment and hopelessness. Do you share her sentiment?

HAVE YOU LOST HOPE?

It seems that the older today's singles grow, the more hopeless about marriage they become. Some, like Annie, have stopped searching for a soul mate altogether. Many say they can believe God has a plan for their education and career—even for the purchase of a car or house—but they have trouble believing that God has a soul mate for them. Some wonder if God has called them to be single and they are just not listening. Have you ever wondered this? Perhaps you have just pushed your desire for a spouse down in utter frustration. If this is the case, then you will want to read on.

THE HEALING JOURNEY IS INWARD

Like Annie, you may be looking outward, sizing up all of the available men and women around you with an extremely critical eye. However, the path to finding a mate and the path to emotional healing is inward, not outward. We encouraged Annie (as we encourage you) to take a look inward and ask the Lord to show her anything that could be standing in the way of finding love.

At first Annie did not want to do this. She wanted to focus only on the "bad" men in her life who she saw through a lens that magnified their flaws. She had a negative attitude toward God because He had not seen fit to bring her a "decent, caring man." She spent a great deal of time in sessions talking about how bad the men in her life were, but did not look at herself in the same evaluative light. While she could not see any of her faults, she was very quick to point out all of theirs. Scripture cautions against this in Matthew 7:3-4: "Why do you look at the speck of sawdust in your brother's eye and pay no attention to the plank in your own eye? How can you say to your brother, 'Let me take the speck out of your eye,' when all the time there is a plank in your own eye?" (NIV). In order to get the "plank" out of her eye, Annie had to take a good look at her family of origin, relationship history, and relational programming and beliefs.

FAMILY OF ORIGIN

Both family of origin (our parents and siblings) and the generations of family members that have gone before us have a significant impact on how we behave in our adult relationships. Our family history consciously and unconsciously programs how we think and feel about love, marriage, life, and even God.

If your family was selfish and withheld love, you might see marriage as a prison and God as cold and aloof. Conversely, if your family was loving, you have a greater likelihood of seeing marriage and God in a more positive light. Family has a profound affect on the development of our faith. If you came from a family that did not or could not meet your needs, then you will struggle with having faith in God's provision.

As you look at your family history, it is important to remember that we are not on a fault-finding mission. The goal is not to blame your family for who you are. In fact, we have a saying in the Soul Healing Love Model that "Blame is not our game." We challenge you to look at the past in order to understand how you've been programmed and learn how to make healthy and informed decisions.

ANNIE'S FAMILY HISTORY

When Annie was sixteen years old, her parents divorced, which was unheard-of in her small Catholic community. Her mother took on a full-time job as a social worker, spending long hours at work to support her eight children. As the oldest, Annie was thrust into the role of surrogate parent to her younger siblings after her parents' divorce. Always responsible and hard working, she adapted to her wounds by becoming a care-taker and a workaholic.

As she looked back, Annie also saw that she harbored anger and resentment toward her father, because he had never affirmed her. He believed that women should bear children rather than pursue careers in a "man's world" and favored Annie's five broth-ers, giving them preference, time, and attention.

Annie's mom fought her husband to go back to school. He resisted. She fought him to get a job as a social worker. He resisted. She asked for help with the eight children as she reentered the workforce. Still, he resisted. This attitude toward women eventu-ally cost him his marriage. Annie's mom got tired of being treated like a maid and a babysitter and finally left. Annie was infuriated and devastated by her father's behavior, which became the root of her distrust and extreme anger toward men.

Medical school further contributed to Annie's poor attitude toward men. All of her chief residents were difficult-to-please men. These Ivy League superiors made it clear that she would have to work harder than her male counterparts in order to compete. She was a talented, capable, and compassionate resi-dent and quickly proved that she could hold her own. However, Annie's anger and resentment toward men continued to grow as she spent years in male-dominated medical schools among people who wanted to keep women "in their place." Annie closed herself off to men, and, inadvertently, to God's provision.

We have found that there are many women who desire a mate but have a deep-seated anger toward men that gets in their way. In addition, many of these women are confused as to just how strong they should be in this day and age. Annie's strong, aggressive style worked well for her career, but if she was too aggressive in dating relationships, men were turned off. Annie's confusion is a direct result of the changing roles of men and women in our culture over the past forty years.

THE CHANGING ROLES FOR WOMEN

In 1963 Betty Friedan wrote *The Feminine Mystique*, which many believe signaled the beginning of the women's movement. Friedan believed that women were relegated to the roles of mother, maid, and laundress in exchange for their living situations with men. She told women that their identities were being stolen from them and that they were not living up to their full potential. Women became dissatisfied with their marriages, and this discontentment was labeled "the housewife's syndrome."

Friedan's book and the ensuing women's movement turned our culture and the Christian community upside down. During this time, a plethora of feminine psychology books appeared, teaching women that they simply did not have to be "thankless caretakers" or "doormats to men." While many of these books helped women recover from codependency and the legacy of male oppression, they commonly cast men as villains. Women began to blame men entirely for their unhappiness, lack of fulfillment, and low self-esteem and divorced their husbands in record numbers. Many of these women lost their faith in men, their faith in marriage, and subsequently their faith in God as the author of matrimony.

This divorce epidemic left many daughters like Annie in its wake. Many of these sons and daughters of the "divorce generation" were so hurt by their parents' divorce that they closed their hearts to each other and to marriage, hence the term "the closed heart syndrome."

THE CLOSED HEART SYNDROME

Susan Jeffers, in her book *Opening Our Hearts to Men*, shares how the women's movement left women angry, closed off, and mistrustful of men. Jeffers says that women have substituted the closed heart syndrome for the housewife syndrome and feel emotionally safer staying single. Jeffers believes the cure for closed heart syndrome does not require women to give up what they have gained in their struggle for identity. Rather, women should open themselves to the possibility that men may have something to add to their lives. She writes,

> When we made an enemy of men we numbed ourselves to the fact that they are human, and in that, their struggle for survival is just as hard for them as it is for us. To keep them the enemy, we have blocked our vision to the pain, fear, and emptiness they so often feel. Even more significantly, our anger has served to mask the truth of what is really going on within ourselves. It has delayed our having to deal with our own pain, fear and emptiness, which even in our well-defended personalities, pops up painfully at times. Ironically, it is from this place of pain that our capacity to empathize and love emerges. I have noticed that those (men and women) most numbed to their own deepest pain can be the cruelest of all.[1]

You may have closed your heart in order to numb your pain, but this will limit your capacity to love and trust others and to trust God for a soul mate.

DO SOUL MATES EXIST?

Like many of today's singles, you may be skeptical about the concept of a soul mate. You may feel that those who believe they have found a soul mate are naive, delusional, or unrealistic. You may say that the idea of a soul mate was cooked up by hopeless romantics to sell novels and promote chick flicks.

Even with this prevailing disillusionment, research shows that many still believe in the concept of a soul mate. Researchers from Rutgers University interviewed single men in four major metropolitan areas and found that the majority of them believed in the idea of a soul mate. In fact, the soul mate ideal was their most desired marital characteristic, surpassing religion, economics, and even the ability to be a good parent. A recent Gallup poll also showed that the majority of singles believe in the possibility of finding in the universe a special someone meant just for them.[2] In other words, a soul mate.

What exactly is a soul mate? Thomas Moore, in his book *Soul Mates*, says,

A soul mate is someone to whom we feel profoundly connected, as though the communication and communing that takes place between us were not a product of internal efforts, but rather divine grace.[3]

Tom and I believe that the concept of a soul mate is not as mystical or ethereal as you might think. We believe that soul mates are formed as well as found. You become soul mates with your husband or wife by doing the hard work of merging two different souls.

When Tom and I met, we were spiritually in tune, our goals and values were compatible, and we had a good amount of attraction and chemistry, which led us both to believe that we could be soul mates. Like many people, we naively believed this would make our relationship easy. But after thirty years, we know that becoming and staying soul mates depends on hard work, not mystical chance.

Our unconscious minds, our body chemistry, and even our parents' influence on our psyches all play significant roles as we choose whom we will date. However, we also believe that God directs His children to a soul mate. Therefore, we encourage you to pray for a helper, a complement, a soul mate. God can surely provide this special someone for you, but first you must surrender your desires to Him. You will have to confront your lack of faith, as well as any pessimism toward members of the opposite sex, as you begin to trust in the Lord's provision.

TRUSTING IN GOD'S PROVISION

Annie, our workaholic surgical resident, said that she could possibly surrender her negative attitude toward men if God would give her a guarantee. She wanted the Lord to lead her to a man who would start their courtship for the explicit purpose of marriage. Who wouldn't want to date with a "no-risk, money-back guarantee"? There is always a certain amount of risk with love, but the Lord asks us to depend on Him to navigate our path. God wanted Annie to take that risk so that she could find a soul mate, but also so that she would trust Him. Her faith could not grow without surrender.

GOD HAS A PLAN

Tom and I can't tell you with absolute certainty that you will marry a particular person on a particular day or even in a particular year. We can tell you that God doesn't give a person the desire to swim, the resources to learn how, and the ability to do it just to send him or her to the desert where there is no water to be found. God does not leave His children hanging. He is not too busy to answer your prayers. He knows exactly what you are going through.

If you desire a soul mate, God understands. Psalm 37:4-5 says,

Delight yourself in the LORD
and he will give you the desires of your heart.

Commit your way to the LORD;

trust him and he will do this. (NIV)

ANNIE'S HEALING

Annie began to pray about what the Lord had for her in the area of dating. She started to recognize and deal with her closed heart syndrome by forgiving the men in her life who had wounded her. As she opened her heart to men, her faith began to grow. She began to trust the Lord through the difficult course of finding her soul mate.

I remember the day she came in for a session after finding out that her ex-boyfriend was engaged. While she had learned a great deal and was more optimistic about the possibility of finding a mate, the shock of this news saddened and discouraged her. She needed a boost in her faith to go on. During her counseling session, a story came to my mind and I felt led to share it with her. It was a story about how Tom and I needed to develop faith in our own lives.

A STORY OF FAITH

About ten years ago, the Lord, along with our clients, strongly encouraged us (more like hounded us) to write a book about the Soul Healing Love Model. We were flattered, but also fearful that no one would publish our work. We began praying but felt afraid and incompetent. This was not the best way to start a mission for the Lord.

I did not know the first thing about getting a book published. My wounds from childhood were rearing their ugly heads and echoing in my psyche. I heard destructive internal self-talk like *You can't write a book. It is too big of a task. There are hundreds of more qualified therapists out there who can write better than you.*

You are just a little hillbilly girl from the Deep South. What could you have to offer in a book? I was a therapist with twenty-five years of experience, but I still wasn't immunized from my childhood soul wounds.

I knew that the Lord had ministered His unconditional love to me, but this was a true test of my trust in His provision. I realized that I had to consciously choose faith rather than fear, optimism rather than doubt. I regularly made a part of my devotional life Hebrews 11:1, which states, "Now faith is the substance of things hoped for, the evidence of things not seen." I had no guarantee that our book would be published, yet I knew the Lord wanted us to write it, if for no other reason than to test my faith. I had to write out of sheer obedience. I had to call publishers out of sheer obedience. I had to subject myself to the possible rejection of my life's work out of sheer obedience.

Are you kidding me, Lord? I have had enough rejection in my life. I don't want any more. Tom and I are doing fine as Christian counselors, so why would you want me to risk rejection again? This is exactly how Annie felt. She was successful as a surgeon and did not want to pursue a relationship that might cause pain and rejection.

The Lord's answer to me, as well as to Annie, was clear. He wanted us to obey. I told Annie that I would obey and risk rejection out of obedience if she would do the same. I would contact publishers if she would try out singles groups in the area. It was hard for me to write and call publishers, but I did it because the Lord wanted me to. He wanted me to hear the plethora of "nos" that plague a first-time author's book proposal. "No, we don't take unsolicited manuscripts." "No, we don't publish first-time authors." "No, we are not interested." Ouch! Did that ever hurt my feelings (and my ego).

I learned two valuable lessons through this process. First, the Lord wanted to teach me obedience and trust. Second, He wanted me to be humbled. Ouch, again! I had become too confident and comfortable in my profession. The Lord wanted me to be a beginner, a freshman, to start anew in order to be totally dependent on His leading. I had forgotten how precious it was for Him to lead my every step. After twenty-five years, I had become so comfortable in the role of therapist that I had a tendency to rely on my own strength rather than His power in my life.

Setting out on this new course of obedience and faith grew both Tom and me like no other journey that we have ever taken. We soon learned how to depend on the Lord for every breath. We had to grit our teeth as we heard the frequent "nos" and hang on to our faith as the rejection letters poured in. God was maturing us, and we needed to trust in His provision knowing that He was with us every step of the way.

ANNIE'S HAPPY ENDING

The Lord was with Annie also as He awakened her longing for a soul mate. Annie humbled herself before the Lord and made a commitment to get out there and date again. She even started going to the "dreaded singles group" at her church, which she had sworn off long ago. She told me that it took sheer obedience to go every Sunday evening, sheer obedience to go up to men and introduce herself, and sheer obedience to attend the social events that the group sponsored.

While it was very difficult for Annie, she met several women who befriended her and invited her to various social events. One woman had season football tickets. Annie didn't like football, but once again, attended out of sheer obedience. At the game she met Peter, who worked with the woman who had invited her. They hit it off immediately. Peter was almost forty and was not actively dating either. He confessed to Annie that he had sworn off singles groups and had all but given up on finding a mate. As it turned out, this was not all they had in common.

Annie and Peter spent the next year getting to know each other. When they came to the point of wanting to date exclusively, they agreed to come to counseling. It was a great privilege and pleasure to talk with Annie and Peter as they planned their future together. Annie and Peter have been married for two years and are happier than they ever could have imagined. And as for us—well, we did find a publisher for our first book and for the others to come. God is indeed faithful.

MAKING IT PRACTICAL: WHAT ABOUT ME?

God has a plan for you, a plan that just might include a soul mate. As you read the rest of this book, begin to pray that the Lord will open you up to His plan, His choices, and His mate for you. Trust Him to do it and He will.

FOR FURTHER THOUGHT

1. Have you, like Annie, ever been angry at God for not giving you a spouse?

2. Do you have an inner anger toward the opposite sex because of hurt you have suffered in the past? Prayerfully examine whether your anger is rooted in unforgiveness and ask God to help you forgive.

3. How has your family history affected your ability to trust in God's provision?

GROWING YOUR FAITH

- God knows my longing for a spouse and wants to give me the desires of my heart.

  Delight yourself also in the LORD,
  And He shall give you the desires of your heart. (Psalm 37:4)

- God is faithful, and I can trust His provision for a soul mate.

> Commit your way to the LORD,
> Trust also in Him. (Psalm 37:5)

- God wants me to humbly depend on Him, not on my own strength.

> Trust in the LORD with all your heart,
> And lean not on your own understanding;
> In all your ways acknowledge Him,
> And He shall direct your paths. (Proverbs 3:5-6)

Unresolved Issues from the Past

I always seem to attract unhealthy people

R on, a thirty-four-year-old singles minister, called us because he needed help with his relationships. It seemed that quite a few women had crushes on him and would not leave him alone. You would think this was a good problem to have, but Ron tended to attract needy, clingy, and emotionally fragile women. These women had been rejected by men in the past and were attracted to Ron because he was warm, caring, and friendly. They were sure that he would not reject them. After all, he was a pastor.

Ron had another dilemma. Some of these women started coming to his singles group, but he did not want to date them because he thought it might be a conflict of interest. When he shared this with the would-be sweethearts, it seemed to have little impact. In fact, it made them more interested.

Ron's warmth and kindness were often mistaken for "interest" by these women, so they called him constantly and sent notes, flowers, and cookies. Two women even claimed that God had told them they were supposed to marry Ron. This created a real predicament for Ron, because he did not hear the same "divine" messages. Ron was attracted to strong, independent women, but they rarely reciprocated his level of affection. He was understandably frustrated. The women he wanted did not want him, and the women he didn't want wouldn't leave him alone.

SALLY'S STORY

Sally was a thirty-five-year-old, attractive fitness instructor who had the opposite problem. She came into our counseling office because she did not have many potential suitors at all. At the time, she was "unofficially" dating Ken, her yardman. She said unofficially, because he never took her out. Their "dates" consisted of his ordering cheap takeout and eating at her place once a week. He did not want to take her to his place because he still lived with his parents (at age thirty-six)!

Deep inside, Sally knew that Ken was immature and not at all ready for marriage. After all, how many thirty-six-year-olds still live at home? However, she thought she might be able to help him out. Ken liked being around such a solid, mature woman, and Sally liked feeling needed. Besides, the guys she really wanted never expressed any interest in her. She had given up on finding someone better, so she continued trying to "improve" Ken.

Sally met a lot of successful, mature men through her job at the health club. Initially they seemed to show interest, but they would quickly cool off and become distant. Sally was confused and hurt. Finally, she asked one lukewarm suitor why he had lost interest so quickly. He told her that she was too intimidating. Sally couldn't understand this. She had never thought of herself as intimidating. She was a good, firm boss who managed a lot of men. Perhaps she had grown a little tough, but only because she had to work so hard to move up the ranks at work. A lot of professional women face this dilemma: they work so hard to develop toughness in a man's world that they become too tough for the men for whom they have adapted.

Sally had never intended to stay in this tough role for so long, but it paid well and she needed to support herself. She was good at what she did, and to be good, she had to be a bit intimidating. All she ever really wanted was to fall in love, marry, and have a family, but this was one goal that she just could not seem to accomplish. She was frustrated and hurt and so she settled for less "just to have a man."

Both Ron's and Sally's relationship problems are common in the singles scene. They thought that their problems were about their suitors or the lack thereof. While some of this might be true, what Ron and Sally did not realize was that there were also internal reasons why they attracted the wrong kind of mates. Unresolved issues from their past stood in the way of finding a healthy soul mate. Ron and Sally were looking outside of themselves to find the answers to their dating difficulties, but the path to emotional and spiritual healing is inward. For this reason, self-awareness and examination were essential.

RESISTANCE

We have found that it is typical for people to resist looking at the past to see how it has affected them. Many wonder how something that happened so many years ago could possibly affect them today. This is a common perception. However, it is important to realize the power of our past on our present. Studies have shown that significant negative events from our past are recorded in the brain and can actually be triggered in adult relationships. Because of this, it is wise to look at your past with an open mind and see how it has impacted you.

Some people avoid looking at their past because they do not want to deal with the pain. We say in the Soul Healing Love

Model, "You can't heal what you can't feel." Recognizing the wounds in your past, feeling the pain, and allowing God to heal you will set you free to become a healthy soul mate, who, in turn, attracts prospective healthy soul mates.

FAMILY HISTORY

In counseling, we typically ask people to give us a detailed family history, which includes questions about the occurrence of divorce, alcoholism, drug addiction, mental illness, and childhood trauma. We do this to help people become aware of the family dynamics in which they were raised and enable them to see what may have been passed down through their family history. We call the wounds that occurred in the past *soul wounds*.

SOUL WOUNDS

A soul wound is a need from childhood that was not met. Childhood soul wounds need to be dealt with or they can reoccur in adulthood and sabotage your love life. Finding healing will prepare you for healthy love. It will also allow you to see a prospective partner's woundedness and need for healing. Instead of looking for love as a wounded person and attracting wounded people, you become a person who is being healed and can be a healing agent to your partner. You also become more likely to attract healthier partners who would be willing to participate in the healing of your soul wounds. This makes for a good lifetime partnership.

CHILDHOOD HURTS

What many people do not know is there is a neurobiological reason why childhood soul wounds can haunt you in adult relationships. When we experience a hurt or trauma in child-hood, the memory is not stored in the new brain or neocortex, which takes in information and makes rational, conscious deci-sions. Instead, the memories of traumatic experiences and soul wounds are stored in the limbic system or the *old brain*.

Some neurobiologists call the old brain the mammalian brain because it is present in all mammals. Others call it the child brain because of its immature, childlike responses to certain stimuli. The old brain is our self-defense reflex. It is a survival mechanism, our knee-jerk, fight-or-flight response to real or perceived danger. Old brain triggers typically cause a person either to attack or to avoid certain situations. During a traumatic period of our life, this behavior may have been necessary, but if we do not work through that trauma, we will continue to react in destructive ways.

The emotional system's or old brain's speed of processing is two hundred to five thousand times faster than thought or language.[1] Because of this, we react very quickly to our old-brain triggers. This is why emotions, if left unchecked, can rule the psyche in unhealthy ways. Also, the old brain is not conscious of time, which means that a memory that occurred at age five can be relived at age twenty-five with the same feeling and emotion experienced at the time of the original trauma. If a soul wound occurs at a young age, it can be triggered again later in life. This can be quite scary for people as they form their adult love rela-tionships. When a soul wound is triggered, a person typically overreacts because he is reliving or reexperiencing feelings from his past. This excessive emotion is called *reactivity*.

AN EXAMPLE OF REACTIVITY

Let's assume that your father was negative, critical, and hard to please. Your father's criticism hurt you as a child, leaving soul wounds that cause you to feel inferior and inadequate, especially when criticized. Now suppose you are dating a man who is a bit particular and likes for things to look nice in his apartment. His fastidious nature causes him to correct you when you are putting away the dishes and give you a lot of instructions about taking out the trash. This reminds you of your critical father.

You may have one of many responses. You may tell him that you appreciate his instructions, but can figure these things out for yourself. You may also overlook it and decide to do things according to his instructions. If his criticism hurts you, causing you to overreact, yell, threaten, accuse, or withdraw and pout, then a soul wound is being triggered, and you are being reactive. Giving the situation more attention, emotion, or anger than it deserves indicates a state of reactivity.

Reactivity is dangerous, because when we feel it, we are not thinking rationally. We are reliving the past with feelings and emotions that belong there, not in the current relationship. We may unconsciously blame our partner for something he or she had no part in. Blame is typically a reactive, childlike response from the limbic system or old brain. It obscures solutions by locking us into the victim mode, where we focus on damage, injury, unfairness, and weakness. In such an environment, true intimacy cannot exist.

When we become aware of our soul wounds and how they have led to reactivity, we can take responsibility for the problem. Responsibility focuses on strength, growth, and creative solutions—not blame and victimization. Doing your soul-healing work also prepares you to heal your prospective partner's soul, as well as find a partner willing and capable of healing yours. Love and marriage become a healing journey rather than a selfish what's-in-it-for-me endeavor.

Assessing soul wounds in your childhood may be difficult. Most people don't have the cognitive ability to remember things that happened before the age of three. Some have few childhood memories even after that point. If this is the case, you may want to rely on interviews with trusted family members to determine what happened to you during this time.

STAGES OF SOCIAL DEVELOPMENT

Harville Hendrix, in his excellent book *Keeping the Love You Find*, says that there are six main stages of social development that need to be successfully accomplished before adulthood. In fact, four of those stages occur before the age of seven. If these developmental stages are not completed successfully, key parts of you may be underdeveloped. This can create problems in your adult relationships, especially in dating and mating.

Soul wounds that occur in the first seven years of life play a particularly significant role in our development because they can leave deep psychological scars and rob us of our true selves. We develop adaptations to these wounds in order to be acceptable in our environment. These adaptations form a "false self" that you show in dating and mating. You may fear that if someone knew the "real you" he or she would not love you. Perhaps you are not even sure who the real you might be.

In order for true intimacy to be established, you have to be known. The false self can cause us to push away from our natural gifts and abilities, inhibiting the establishment of true intimacy. We are left only with fractured parts of our authentic selves, broken pieces in need of repair. To quote Hendrix,

> Socialization, then is essentially a process of mutilation, of chipping away at our wholeness.... Fearing our essential

aliveness, we become stick figures, unrecognizable shadows of our unique and joyful selves. What's left is a cobbled up hodgepodge of defenses and adaptations, interspersed with what remains of our true selves.[2]

When we try to date and mate with our fractured selves, we want our partners to complete us. We want them to make us feel whole. It becomes their job to repair the damage and fill the holes in our souls. Not only is this unfair to our prospective partners, it is impossible.

In the movie *Jerry McGuire*, the lead character, played by Tom Cruise, comes to his senses and begs his former girlfriend to come back into his life. The classic romantic line was, "You complete me." You could hear every hopeless romantic in the theater give a resounding, "Awww." Now, this might work in Hollywood, but not in the real world. No one should have the responsibility of "completing you" but the Lord. If Tom and I wrote the script we would have the hero get therapy to fill in some of the missing pieces before embarking on a lifetime commitment with a woman. Expecting a prospective partner to heal our childhood wounds puts entirely too much pressure on that person and will sabotage the relationship.

In order to become aware of our childhood wounds, we can look at each of the six stages of social development and see when and how we were wounded. The wounds that occurred in one or more of these stages may have caused you to adapt in extreme ways and date and mate with a false self. In love relationships, you may overly desire connection or fear connection and become distant and aloof. Take a look at these six stages and ask the Lord to show you the wounds that may have occurred.

STAGE ONE: ATTACHMENT

The first stage of social development is the attachment stage, which starts at birth and goes to the age of eighteen months. The child's developmental task during this period is to form an attachment bond with his or her parents. A seemingly easy task, yet there can be obstacles to the establishment of this bond. Physical separation from the parents or a parent's distressed physical or emotional state may inhibit the bonding process. If the need for attachment is not met in childhood, we may believe later in life that we are unlovable or flawed. If we do not work through these feelings, we can become too attached and clingy or distant and avoidant in adult relationships.

In short, we will either be a *clinger* or an *avoider.* What we want with all of our hearts is to love and be loved, yet this causes so much angst that we have a hard time embracing it. Getting the love we so desperately want scares us to death. It arouses all of our suspicions and anxieties. It is both desired and feared because unconditional love is so unfamiliar to us. Recognizing wounds that may have occurred in the attachment stage can help us heal our fear, and change the tendency to cling too tightly or avoid true intimacy.

STAGE TWO: EXPLORATION

The next developmental stage is the exploration stage, which occurs from eighteen months to age three. The main purpose of this passage is for us, as toddlers, to explore our environment while feeling safe in the security of our parents' or caretakers' presence. During the exploration stage, we move away from the attachment figure and investigate new experiences and relationships. Failure to do this causes us to become suspicious and fearful in love relationships. According to Harville Hendrix, we can adapt to wounds in the exploration stage by becoming either *pursuers*, who chase people in dating relationships, or *isolators*, who are untrusting, reserved, and detached.[3]

Tammy's Wound in the Exploration Stage of Development

We worked with a young woman named Tammy who was abandoned by her father during the exploration stage. Her mother then had a nervous breakdown and was hospitalized. Subsequently, two-year-old Tammy was passed from relative to relative for a year until her mother returned home. She had few memories of these events and had to rely mostly on what her family told her.

Tammy realized that this experience caused her to adapt by becoming a pursuer in love relationships. She tried too hard to please others, and tolerated unhealthy behaviors, even abuse, from her partners. She had a great deal of reactivity around real or perceived abandonment and would not explore the possibility of a new relationship. Her fear kept her trapped in a cycle of remaining loyal to unhealthy men who did not deserve it. When Tammy understood the connection of her present behavior to her past, she began to heal and develop healthy boundaries in her dating relationships.

STAGE THREE: IDENTITY

The identity stage occurs from the ages of three and four. This is a critical stage of personal development; in it we begin to formulate our concept of self and to know who we are apart from our caretakers. This process is called *individuation*. At this stage we assert a lot of "me-ness" and frequently say things like: "This is mine." "I have this." "I want this." These types of statements help us form an idea of who we are as individuals in the world.

In order for us to successfully complete the identity stage, we need to develop a stable, consistent internal image of ourselves and our caretakers. During this stage, we try out new behaviors like mimicking the personalities of those in our environment and emulating superheroes. The affirmation we receive from our parents helps us develop a clear and distinct identity. Failure to receive this affirmation can lead to deep insecurities regarding self worth and self-esteem.

Wounds in this stage cause us to adapt in two extreme ways: We may become *controllers*, who are critical, domineering, and rigid, or *diffusers*, who are submissive and compliant.[4]

STAGE FOUR: COMPETENCE

The competence stage occurs from the ages of four to seven. The purpose of this stage is to experiment by testing our skills and challenging our aptitudes and abilities, while seeking praise from our parents. According to Dr. Hendrix, if we do not complete this developmental task, a feeling of incompetence may haunt us later in life. We can adapt by becoming either *competitors* or, the other extreme, *compromisers*.[5]

As competitors, we may perform and compete to gain approval. In dating relationships, we present our résumé of accomplishments to prospective partners and peruse theirs to see if they can meet our dating standards. Competitors are always right, always inflexible, and always, well, competitive.

The other extreme of the adaptation continuum is the compromiser. Too sweet, too passive, they act victimized and powerless and often manipulate to get their way. Compromisers let others take the lead in relationships, and sacrifice what they want in order to be loved. Ron, the minister you read about at the beginning of the chapter, was a compromiser.

STAGE FIVE: SOCIAL CONCERN

The fifth stage of social development, the social concern stage, occurs from the ages of seven to twelve. For many, this stage ends during the tumultuous junior high or middle school years. Virtually no one has escaped early adolescence without being wounded during this stage. Teasing is predominant. Anyone who is different is ostracized. This is the stage where we develop crushes on the opposite sex, which may lead to painful rejection. It is the time for "puppy love," but also the time for crushed egos and broken hearts. This stage of development can be a veritable storehouse of unresolved issues, as rejection and soul wounding is almost inevitable.

Hendrix states that if we are wounded in the social concern stage of development, we can withdraw and become *loners*, unconsciously vowing not to get emotionally close to others, or *caretakers*, whose invasive, intrusive, and overly eager-to-please style causes partners to feel smothered.[6]

Rachel's Wound in the Social Concern Stage of Development

Rachel was an example of someone who was wounded in the social concern stage. She had been married twice and both of her husbands had cheated on her and left the marriage. When she came into counseling, she had been dating a man for only two months, yet complained that he did not spend enough time with her and refused to match her level of commitment to the relationship. She whined to him about how much time he spent at work and how she felt left out when he was with his children. When she did spend time with him, she acted too familiar, too soon. She cooked for him and his two sons, mowed his lawn, and picked up his dry cleaning in hopes that he would love her and keep her around.

Rachel's "boyfriend" took full advantage of her kindness and loyalty but still did not spend a great deal of time with her. He would not commit to being exclusive, but reaped the benefits of an exclusive relationship. This frustrated her, but instead of setting boundaries, she tried harder and did more to try to please him. He thought she was suffocating him. She thought he was distant and noncommittal. In counseling, it became obvious that she had been wounded at age thirteen (the social concern stage), when her brother started taking drugs and became an addict. Rachel had adapted to this wound by becoming a caretaker.

STAGE SIX: INTIMACY

The last stage of social development is the intimacy stage, which starts at age thirteen and goes to age nineteen. This is the stage where adolescence blooms into young adulthood. This is typically when we find our first love. If the relationship ends in heartbreak, it can hinder your ability to love in a healthy way.

The purpose of this stage is to develop intimacy skills. It is where most of our ideas about love and intimacy are formed. Many young girls form their idea of love from romance novels and teen movies or chick flicks. Young men learn about love from tough-guy action thrillers, locker-room talk, and, unfortunately, pornography. This can wreak havoc with the formation of a teenager's understanding of intimate relationships, causing singles to have a perception of love that is not realistic.

If you are wounded in the intimacy stage of social development, you will adapt by becoming a *rebel* or a *conformist*. Rebels fear being controlled, do not like to be told what to do, and do not want to grow up. Conformists on the other hand, do not want to be different, tend to impose their rules on others, and can be self-righteous and judgmental.[7]

If you were wounded in any of these six stages of social development, you may have adapted in unhealthy ways, which are still affecting you today. It would be a good idea to create a timeline of your development and list the significant events that happened to you during your first fifteen years of life. This will help you determine what soul wounds might have occurred and their present effect. The singles we read about in the beginning of the chapter saw that their wounds in key stages caused them to have difficulty in forming healthy, intimate relationships.

RON'S STORY

We encouraged Ron to look at what happened to him in these stages of development in order to understand his dating and mating behaviors. He was the third of four sons. His father was a successful, well-known attorney who built his law practice when Ron was a child. He had little time for Ron during his early years. When Ron was five years old (the competency stage), his dad became senior partner. He worked nights and weekends, stopped going on family outings and vacations, and seldom went to church with his family.

During that time, Ron began to play baseball. His dad did not have time to come to his games or play catch. Ron internalized his father's absence as rejection, which left him feeling unworthy and terribly incompetent. The more we internalize a message like this, the more we generalize it in our lives. For Ron this meant that the more unworthy and incompetent he felt as a little boy, the more he generalized this feeling as a young man.

Ron adapted to his wounds by becoming a compromiser who was sweet, passive, and too eager to please. Because of this, he tended to pick women who were his opposite in order to feel whole and complete. (Apparently, he and Jerry McGuire had some things in common.) Ron was attracted to strong, competent, independent women who were competitors.

Unfortunately, these competitive women unconsciously made him feel incompetent. They picked up his unconscious and conscious passivity, and pulled away. This caused him to try harder and perform even more. He was caught in a repetition compulsion that was destroying his chances for intimacy. The more he was rebuffed, the harder he performed, the more incompetent he felt.

REPETITION COMPULSION

Repetition compulsion, a concept first detailed by Sigmund Freud, is the tendency to repeat patterns in life that are familiar to our unconscious memory. Freud believed we have an unconscious need to reproduce the environment of our childhood, hoping to impact it differently so that the outcome will change. If developmental stages are not completed successfully, repetition compulsions can be quite potent. Most of the time, the pattern yields the same results and serves only to reinforce the original wound.

According to Harville Hendrix's Imago relationship theory, we are attracted to people who are like our parents or primary caretakers, which is also a form of repetition compulsion. We are attracted to them because we feel like these people have the potential to heal our childhood wounds and give us the love we have always wanted. This explains why, when we fall in love, we feel an almost mystical familiarity and comfortableness around that person. The feeling *I have known you all my life* is part of our unconscious instinct trying to heal our woundedness. Hendrix calls this *the phenomenon of recognition*.[8] The familiar, unconscious desire for healing is the driving force behind love relationships. This was the case with Ron.

RON'S HEALING

Ron continually tried to perform to win the approval of competitive, strong women who were a lot like his father. These women had no need or desire to take care of an insecure man and rebuffed him. Some women even said that he was too nice or tried too hard, which further reinforced his feelings of incompetence.

During his early years, when his dad was at work, Ron spent a lot of time with his mom, who taught him to develop his compassionate, caring side. This further pushed him to become a compromiser. He needed a dad for balance. He needed a dad to teach him how to be a man. His mother taught him to be warm and caring and meet women's needs, which caused him to be a magnet for needy, clingy, wounded women. He felt competent with these women and presented his best, most-caring self.

Unfortunately, with women who were stronger, he felt inferior and incompetent. With the help of the Holy Spirit, he began to reprogram his belief system and believe he was worthy of a competent, strong, independent wife. This newly developed confidence caused him to set better boundaries with needy women in his congregation and to become attractive to healthier, stronger women.

It was not long after he made these changes in his life that he met Alisha, who was also a minister. She was strong, healthy, and competent—just the type of woman who had once made Ron feel inferior. But because Ron was resolving his childhood wounds, he had a newfound confidence that enabled him to pursue a relationship with Alisha. They were married fifteen months later. If Ron had not resolved the issues from his past, he might be single to this day.

SALLY'S HEALING

As Sally, the fitness instructor, began to look at the soul wounds in her life, she also realized that she had unresolved issues from her past. Her parents divorced when she was sixteen years old, wounding her in the social concern stage. Sally watched her mother's financial status drop drastically while her dad dated younger women. She went from living in an upper middle class family to existing on a meager amount of child support. Her mom was too depressed to work and her dad was too interested in his girlfriends to pay much attention to her. Sally knew at a tender age that she was on her own physically and emotionally. She was forced to become independent and self-sufficient. She got a job to help out the family's financial situation, took care of her mom, and made excellent grades.

She had always been a driven child, but after the divorce she had a burning desire to succeed in order to earn enough to be able to take care of herself. In counseling, she realized that she had a fear of ending up in the same situation as her mother: abandoned, depressed, and penniless.

These fears fueled her extreme drive and independence, which intimidated many suitors. She was not trying to be intimidating, but the soul wounds she sustained in the social concern stage of development caused her to be a loner and produced an inability to be vulnerable to men. She would not allow herself to need anything from a man, so she appeared aloof, distant, and yes, intimidating.

Sally's soul wounds caused her to have a great deal of reactivity to men. She formed several negative false beliefs that ruled her dating life: *Don't depend on men; they will let you down. Always be capable of taking care of yourself. Don't ask a man to do something for you that you can do yourself. Don't trust or be vulnerable to men, or they will abandon you.* Though her heart desired connection and love, these toxic messages caused her to push men away.

Sally realized that she was unconsciously viewing all men like her father and started replacing this false belief with the truth that not all men were like him. About this time, she and Ken, her impoverished lawn guy, took a permanent break from their relationship. Sally believed that there were good men out there who could be respected and trusted, so she began to change her behavior. She became warmer and more open, which made her less intimidating and more attractive to men.

Not long after we met Sally, she met a laid-back, caring

architect named John. Sally worked hard on her reactivity about John's attempts to get close to her. She shared with him the pain that occurred in her past and how hard she had worked to resolve it. John also had wounds from his past that he was able to share with her. They learned to trust each other and communicate openly and honestly in order to be healing to one another.

After attending a Soul Healers Couples Weekend, Sally and John got engaged. They are doing well and, at the time of this writing, plan to marry within the year. In one of their premarital counseling sessions Sally said with joy, "I'm so glad that I did not give up on finding the person that God had for me. I am so happy! I could not imagine my life without John. And to think that if I had not looked at my past, I would still be eating cheap takeout with poor Ken."

MAKING IT PRACTICAL: WHAT ABOUT ME?

What is God saying to you? Are there soul wounds from the past that might be keeping you from developing healthy love relationship skills? Take some time and ask Him to show you what these wounds might be and how He can heal them. Trust Him to help you, and He will.

FOR FURTHER THOUGHT

1. Make a timeline of your life from ages one to fifteen. What soul wounds occurred during this time?

2. What stage of development did these soul wounds occur in? How did you adapt (for example, by becoming a competitor or a compromiser)?

3. How have your adaptations affected the way you date and mate today? Are there things you can do to make your dating life healthier?

GROWING YOUR FAITH

- God knows the pain I've suffered and wants to heal my soul wounds.

  "I will restore health to you
  And heal you of your wounds," says the LORD. (Jeremiah 30:17)

- I no longer have to be enslaved to my past.

  Now we look inside, and what we see is that anyone united with the Messiah gets a fresh start, is created new. The old life is gone; a new life burgeons! (2 Corinthians 5:17, MSG)

- God can help me to become a healthy person who attracts healthy people.

  "For I am the LORD who heals you." (Exodus 15:26)

Confusion About the Rules

I don't even know how to date

Nancy was a thirty-two-year-old outgoing, energetic computer programmer who came into our counseling office because she needed help with her love life. Her six-year relationship with her college boyfriend had ended, leaving her broken-hearted and depressed. She had spent the last year doing things in her church singles group, and when she felt brave enough to reenter the dating scene, the rules had changed so much that she did not know what to do.

"Who is supposed to take the lead?" she asked. "What are the rules? Do we both pay for dates? How do I know if a guy is interested in me as just a friend or as a possible romantic partner?"

To further complicate matters, no one in her singles group dated. They all just hung out together in small coed groups and socialized. In Bible studies they shared personal information and prayed for each other. On weekends they planned social events or small group functions. The group went on several retreats a year, where they spent long hours together, sharing emotionally and spiritually.

Nancy was on the group leadership team with Kent, a deeply spiritual man who seemed to really mesh with her. They talked for hours on the phone, shared stories about their families, hopes, and dreams, and prayed for each other regularly. Nancy loved this, but she was confused. The closer she got to Kent, the more she started to like him. She even thought that he might be a potential soul mate, but she didn't know how he felt.

Nancy asked us to speak at her group's annual beach retreat. Before one session, Nancy sat on the floor at Kent's feet as he gave her a neck rub. One newcomer to the group assumed that they were a couple and asked Kent how long he and Nancy had been dating. "Oh, we're not dating," was Kent's astonished and somewhat embarrassed response. He quickly tried to clarify the woman's misperception and defensively said, "Nancy and I are just really good friends." The puzzled woman walked away. What this newcomer thought was obvious was not the reality of the situation at all. She was not the only one confused by Kent's ambiguous behavior. Nancy was quite perplexed. One minute Kent was rubbing her shoulders in a quasi-affectionate way, and the next he was denying any romantic connection.

During the retreat, Nancy pulled me aside and poured her heart out about how frustrated she was. She was afraid to share her feelings for fear it would scare him away, so she held back and suffered in silence.

SURROGATE SOUL MATES

Nancy and Kent had become what we call surrogate soul mates. They shared emotionally and spiritually in an open and very deep manner, but without accountability or commitment. Kent did not have to declare his feelings because he got many of the benefits of a close relationship without commitment or the risk of getting hurt. This was not healthy. It was wonderful that they had grown so close, but for their relationship to grow in integrity, they needed accountability.

At our suggestion, Nancy and Kent had the frightening "DTR," or Define the Relationship talk. Kent was shocked that Nancy was confused about his intentions and needed clarity. He did not know what to say, so he told her that he would "pray about it." Nancy felt that Kent was putting her off, but she was glad that they had at last addressed the issue.

After their difficult conversation, Kent began to call less frequently. He missed church and did not tell anyone in the group (including Nancy) that he planned to visit out-of-town friends for the weekend. Nancy was hurt because Kent, who had never done such a thing before, seemed to be running from her. This kind of withdrawal after an emotional encounter is common for men. It was a long and agonizing two weeks before she heard from him.

At last, Kent called, and he and Nancy decided to pray that the Lord would show them what to do with their relationship. They both agreed to seek the Lord and move forward as He guided them. However, Kent went right back to his passive behavior. He did not pursue Nancy or make any type of commitment, but he wanted to hang out, have deep talks, and be close physically and emotionally.

A surrogate soul mate relationship is not healthy because we become more connected and intimate with the surrogate than is appropriate for the relationship. It can also encumber the search for a true soul mate. Singles often get into these nebulous relationships because they do not know how to date. They languish in a sea of ambiguity because the rules have changed.

Dating was not always this vague. My grandpa declared his intentions to date my grandma by asking her parents if he could "call on" her. She, in turn, stood on her courting porch in Tennessee and dropped a handkerchief in front of him as a sign that she was also interested. My grandma kept that hanky until the day she died. There was no ambiguity or uncertainty about my grandparents' intentions. What's happened to our culture? How have we strayed so far, and, more importantly, can we remedy this problem?

As a former sociologist (this was my undergraduate major), I wanted to study courting in the past to see how and why we got off track. I wanted to pick up the good in courting rituals and encourage singles to reestablish some of those habits today. Granted, times have changed, and many of those rituals are no longer plausible. Still, merging some of the past with the present helped us establish a way of dating and mating that we call *intentional dating*. But first, let's explore together the history of courting rituals and try to see where and how we lost our way.

THE HISTORY OF COURTSHIP

In the past, men were much more demonstrative and open about their intentions. If a man asked a woman out on a date, he was interested in her as a romantic partner, and possible spouse. The woman was required by the laws of etiquette to let him take the lead. Courting was much more clearly defined; each partner knew the rules and followed them.

Ellen K. Rothman, in her book *Hands and Hearts: A History of Courtship in America*, studies the diaries and letters of women and men from between 1770 and 1920 to determine courting attitudes and procedures. Rothman writes,

> While men labored over elaborate, self-conscious exposi-
> tions on romantic love, women's responses tended to be
> apologetic, brief and at times almost impersonal in tone....
> The fact that males were more expansive correspondents in
> this period reflects the prevailing stereotypes of men and
> women.[1]

Wow, have things changed! Modern men are much more fearful to pen such eloquent prose about their romantic intentions. Several of the female members of our focus groups read the letters Dr. Rothman collected and swooned as they saw the way these men unabashedly expressed their desires.

Many women today (including Nancy) say that they have to guess at men's intentions because many of the men they know are indecisive and passive. We found a more humorous look at this frustrating plight in an uncommon place: an advertisement for Fannie May Candy on a senior citizens website.[2]

DIFFERENCES IN COURTING RITUALS: THE 1900s VERSUS THE 2000s

1900: The courting call was a complicated event. One had to observe the appropriate amount of time between invitation and actual visit.

2000: "Maybe I'll drop by later."

1900: It was extremely important to conduct a proper discussion on only a small amount of topics, all of which covered the man's interests but nothing too personal.

2000: "Hand me the remote for the game, hon."

1900: Men sent absurdly romantic letters, gushing such scribes as, "A thousand kisses for you," and "Forever yours."

2000: "E-mail me."

1900: It was customary for a local older woman to serve as a matchmaker for young couples. This woman was well known and well regarded in her town or village and garnered much respect from her peers and their offspring.

2000: Match.com.

1900: Parlor games were common and usually played with the chaperone.

2000: Couples spend their time working out at the gym.

1900: Men had to go out of their way and spend a great deal of their wages to bring their young ladies a gift of chocolate, a symbol of love.

2000: www.fanniemay.com.

THE RITUAL OF "CALLING"

The Fannie May candy people gave us a good look at the ritual of "calling." Until the early twentieth century, male suitors would ask a young woman's parents' permission to call on her. If the girl and her family approved of the suitor, they would grant the request, and a time for the call would be set. Beth Bailey, in her book *From Front Porch to Back Seat*,[3] writes about the ritual of calling. The young suitor would typically be received in the family's parlor to talk, meet the girl's parents, have some refreshments, play parlor games, or listen to her play the piano. Calling forced men to be proactive in courtship. While our culture may not want to go back to such a meticulous system, a more deliberate way of dating could solve many problems for today's singles.

The system of calling also involved a great deal of parental input. Our culture values independence, thus parental influence is not considered as important today. However, research shows that couples who have the support of parents and family have a better chance of making their relationship work.

By the mid-1920s calling became less practical as families moved into urban areas where they did not have parlors in which to entertain. In addition, singles began to express more vehemently a desire for the freedom to choose a mate. The idea of "falling in love" gained momentum and cultural acceptability, and a new word appeared on the courtship horizon: "date."

The increasingly widespread availability of the automobile in the 1930s gave young people freedom and mobility. As a result, meetings with parents were replaced by dates with peers. Quiet talks on the front porch were replaced by conversations at the soda shop, and the parlor was exchanged for restaurants and movie theaters. However, with this newfound freedom came responsibility. It was clearly the man's job to ask the woman for a date, and he was expected to pay for everything. Some men in Rothman's writings expressed resentment that they had to do all the work and actually pay for female companionship. It seems it was much easier and cheaper for them when parents made all of the arrangements and provided the food and entertainment. I have often wondered if this resentment contributed to the deterioration of the man's role in dating. It could also be responsible for some of the passivity in today's men, who may desire romance but feel indignant about having to initiate it.

RECREATIONAL DATING

In the 1950s, dating became casual, recreational, and took on a "shopping" feel. Singles were released from the pressure of having to choose a lifelong mate. Advice columnists wrote about the new "dating and rating" system of popularity and told singles that if they dated a lot, they would be considered popular and a "desirable catch." Relationship gurus wrote to single women, instructing them to "get all the dates that you can, make sure your dance card is full, and go only once around the dance floor with a man." Men were encouraged to be "smooth" and have "a good line."

This era supported phoniness, and eventually singles tired of keeping up appearances. They wanted something more genuine. Unfortunately, this led them in the wrong direction.

THE SEXUAL REVOLUTION

The tumultuous 1960s signaled the sexual revolution. These bohemian youth were on a quest for something more real, but they ushered in a reality that was not based on accountability. Their touting of "free love" turned the dating scene to a sexual playground; promiscuity and premarital sex increased drastically. Cohabitation has been steadily on the rise over the past four decades, increasing 864 percent since 1960.[4]

The advent of coed dorms allowed young men and women to achieve a new level of familiarity on college campuses. Girls no longer waited by the hall phone to see if their suitors would call. Men no longer nervously clutched corsages in the parlor of the girl's dorm.

Author Beth Bailey writes of her days as a young college student living in one of the first coed dormitories:

> In search for freedom, honesty, love and equality... we have found only meaningless sex, loneliness, and lack of commitment. We have an epidemic of teen pregnancy and sexually transmitted diseases. Some critics say we have left youth without rules that are essential for stability, much less romance.[5]

Bailey is right. With the increase of freedom and independence came the loss of accountability and innocence. As our society moves toward the way of sin instead of godliness, our dating culture pays the price. Singles like Nancy and Kent are suffering because of it. In a search for less formality and pretentiousness, we've created a culture rampant with one-night stands and uncertainty. This confusion was the beginning of the battle between men and women to equalize power in the dating system.

A MORE EQUAL DATING SYSTEM

Until the sexual revolution, men were clearly the initiators of romantic relationships. Women saw this as an inequity and began to seek independence in a more equal dating system. They did not want to owe men, be obligated to them, or wait for them to make the first move. Men no longer wanted to carry the financial burden or have the pressure and responsibility of always initiating. Can you see why Christian singles are confused about how to date?

HANGING OUT: THE NEW DATING RITUAL

In response to their confusion, singles once again changed the process of dating. Just as calling was replaced by dating, dating has been largely replaced by "hanging out." Hanging out allows singles to go into a group and mingle with prospective mates without defining or taking responsibility for the relationship. Singles can get to know members of the opposite sex casually before deciding whether there is any interest in dating.

From our focus groups, we hear positive things about hanging out, such as:

- "You don't have to be open about your intentions."
- "It takes the pressure off."
- "It is cheaper for men because they do not have to pay for everything."

Opponents of hanging out say things like the following:

- "No one knows the rules so it is hard to know what is really going on."
- "It keeps people from being honest and defining the relationship."

- "The boundaries of the relationship are too blurred."

At first, hanging out was a good thing for Kent and Nancy. It gave them a chance to get to know each other without pressure. However, it was starting to become detrimental. They were able to hide their true feelings and didn't have to be clear about their intentions. Kent could be close one day and pull back the next.

A MOVE BACK TO COURTSHIP

In some Christian circles, there has been a movement to return to a more serious, parent-supervised way of courtship. Josh Harris, in his book *I Kissed Dating Goodbye*, writes about returning to a more traditional means of courting, where dating is done only if intended or ordained by God and solely for the purpose of marriage. Harris thinks this might eliminate some of the role confusion and prevent much of the angst of relationships.

As relationship therapists and parents of two daughters in their twenties, we thought this sounded like a good idea. We watched our daughters try to navigate the sea of dating relationships and saw how confused they were by what a guy meant by his attention and affection. We joked that perhaps it would be easier for our entire family to hire a matchmaker and arrange their marriages. This could at least keep them from misunderstandings and hurt feelings.

However, our nation's singles are unlikely to cooperate with this move back to a parent-involved form of courtship. Throughout history, singles have struggled with wanting more freedom to pick their own mates. Arranged marriages are not the answer to today's confusion about the rules of dating and neither is "kissing dating goodbye."

One of the things we have learned from watching our daughters is that amid all the misunderstandings and hurt feelings, there are powerful lessons that may be learned only in the context of dating. In fact, the Lord has used many of these dating experiences to help them comprehend His unconditional love. Singles could miss out on some of these lessons if they do not date. In fact, some singles actually need to date. Painfully shy singles often need the experience of dating in order to come out of their shells. Socially immature people may need to date to learn how to relate to others. Naive singles need to date to determine what kind of person they should marry.

Another problem with the more serious, traditional means of courtship is that when singles focus too much on finding a spouse, every encounter becomes an audition for marriage. This puts too much pressure on the couple and can cause the relationship to self-destruct. Some singles who court this way announce their desire to date someone by saying these compelling, and often terrifying words, "God has told me that you will be my husband (or wife)." Wow. That's heavy for a first date.

I actually had a guy say this to me in college. It scared me to death because the Lord had not spoken to me at all about marrying him. I did not even feel led to date him. It felt like manipulation or, even worse, spiritual extortion. Later, I had a long talk with my singles pastor. My pastor told me he thought that this young man was afraid of being rejected so he was using God as "clout" to ensure that I would say yes. But he was sadly mistaken. The Lord had a handsome Californian in mind for me.

Sometimes singles use the move toward traditional courtship as an excuse to stop dating altogether, especially if they have just suffered from a painful breakup. They give up on dating because they don't want to be hurt. Many of these singles then act like surrogate soul mates in order to have their emotional needs met. Kent's giving Nancy a neck rub was entirely too chummy for "just friends." Kent needed to be open about his feelings, declare his intentions, and take the lead.

WOMEN WANT MEN TO LEAD

In our focus groups, we always ask the question: "What would make dating a better experience?" The majority of the women say things like "We want men to take the lead! We want to be pursued." There has been a great deal of damage done by their "liberated" foremothers who have inadvertently stopped this from happening.

Men were designed by God to be the leaders, but they have stepped back. Women, in their impatience, have stepped up. While some men in our focus groups say that it takes the pressure off for women to be the initiators in relationships, they also say it is a turnoff if women are too aggressive. It can create confusion for both genders. Author and family therapist Augustus Napier spoke about this confusion during a meeting of the American Association of Marital and Family Therapists:

> The fact is that the winds of change blowing through the lives of so many women today are shaking up their partners, who are still mostly reacting — and reacting negatively. Few men have a new sense of direction and purpose, which is related to roles. We know the right words to say about equality these days, but are clearly on the defensive; and we could use whatever is at hand to resist change. . . . Our culture is awash with disillusionment with men, and for good reason. . . . In fact, on that wonderful forum for American absurdity, Saturday Night Live, a mythic pop psychology writer — addressed completely in black — was recently found promoting her book, 'Woman Good, Man Bad,' in which all her martyred heroines were the victims of men.[6]

As we attended this conference, we know that after the resounding laughter, Dr. Napier received a standing ovation.

Why do men have so much trouble catching up to the brave new women that Dr. Napier talked about in his speech? Why do these women tell us they do not feel as brave as they once did? Could it be that they are confused about the rules of dating?

A BETTER WAY TO DATE

Clearly, things need to change. We need a better way to date. Generations X and Y tell us that "kissing dating goodbye" and courting solely with the intention of marriage is too serious, and recreational dating or hanging out is much too trivial. We advocate *intentional dating*.

INTENTIONAL DATING

Intentional dating is a balanced cross between the marriage-focused courtship of the past and the casual, recreational dating of the present. Intentional daters allow their family and friends to provide input into their dating and mate selection, but they do not depend entirely on them. They have a deliberate, conscious mind-set about dating and mating. Now don't misunderstand us. Intentional daters are not always on the hunt for a mate or singularly focused on dating every time they are in a coed group. They are merely mindful of what God might be doing in their lives. Here are some of the characteristics of intentional daters:

Healthy. Intentional daters know they are hardwired for love and do not push away from this God-given desire. They work to develop a healthy self-esteem because they know that the way to find a healthy person is to be one. The intentional dater embodies the saying that "healthy people *know* who they are, *like* who they are, and *are* who they are."

Conscious. Intentional daters have done a solid

self-examination; they have looked at their fears of dating and mating and surrendered them to God. They are committed to being genuine and sincere as they pursue members of the opposite sex.

Men Lead and Women Let Them. Men are deliberate and initiate relationships but welcome strong, powerful women who want to be involved in the process. In short, men take their rightful, God-inspired place in relationships. Women overcome their struggle with "owing men" or "feeling obligated" and allow men to take the lead. They are honest and show integrity by truthfully approaching the person they are dating if they sense that he is resistant to leadership. This takes a sincere, truthful, yet tempered, approach to men.

Courageous. Intentional daters have faced their fear of rejection head on, given up destructive habits, and faced the risk of heartbreak. Intentional daters believe that the Lord has a soul mate for them and develop the faith that He will provide. They trust God to lead them in pursuing their heart's desire for a mate.

Integrity of Intentions. Problems often arise in dating relationships when people don't take responsibility for the relationship or are unsure of a person's intentions. Intentional daters make every effort to have integrity in all of their relationships. With God's help, they speak the truth and honor each other as much as they possibly can.

Respectful. Intentional daters respect the person they are dating as a child of God. They do not view members of the opposite sex as conquests or a means to an end.

Authentic. Intentional daters are real. They do not play games or deceive others in dating or mating. There is a problem here, however. What if an authentic dater cannot find members of the opposite sex who are also authentic?

Inevitably, when we speak to singles, we are asked, "What if I am an intentional dater and there are not intentional daters out there to choose from?" Our answer is not an easy one to accept. Be patient and wait for the Lord to work. If the Lord is helping you to be real and honest, then He is probably preparing your mate.

Another common question is, "What if I start to become authentic and the person I am seeing can't handle it?" Once again the answer is not particularly palatable. Stay strong. Be authentic and honest even when it causes a reluctant man (or woman) to withdraw. It is impossible to force another person to be real, but it is valid to point out his or her fear and hesitation in a real and honest fashion.

If the person you are dating wants to have a surrogate relationship, take a prayerful look at that relationship and set healthy boundaries. If there is no pursuit, if your relationship is vague or ambiguous, your partner is probably not really interested. Listen to God, and be strong and courageous. Intentional daters do not continue in a relationship that is not legitimate just to avoid being alone.

NANCY AND KENT'S HAPPY ENDING

Kent and Nancy saw that they were not moving forward with their relationship because they did not want to risk being vulnerable. As Kent learned about intentional dating, he saw that it was his responsibility to take the lead with Nancy.

Though he was scared, Kent began to pray for wisdom and surrendered his fear to the Lord. He began to share his true feelings with integrity, which gave Nancy the courage to be open with him. Finally, they both felt they could move ahead in their relationship. As they shared their hearts with each other and practiced intentional dating, a deep love started to grow between them. From time to time, they would get confused and revert to their old unhealthy patterns, but they worked through this and continued to stay the course. Nancy loved Kent's newfound strength as a leader—so much that she took him up on his offer to lead her for the rest of her life.

MAKING IT PRACTICAL: WHAT ABOUT ME?

Perhaps you, like Kent and Nancy, are confused about the rules of dating. You may have gotten comfortable hiding your true feelings. Maybe the rules have changed so much that you don't even try to date anymore. Take some time to pray and ask the Lord to show you how He wants you to date and mate. Trust Him to help you, and He will.

FOR FURTHER THOUGHT

1. What are the strengths and weaknesses of dating in today's world? Are you ever confused by the rules or lack thereof?

2. Have you, like Kent and Nancy, ever been in a surrogate soul mate relationship? Was it ever a source of frustration?

3. Review the characteristics of intentional dating. What characteristics do you need to work on in order to become a healthy dater?

GROWING YOUR FAITH

- I will show integrity by having appropriate boundaries in my relationships.

    Love doesn't strut,
    Doesn't have a swelled head,
    Doesn't force itself on others,
    Isn't always "me first." (1 Corinthians 13:4-5, MSG)

- I will respect myself and others as children of God.

  "But remember the root command: Love one another." (John 15:17, MSG)

- I will be clear in my intentions toward the opposite sex and take responsibility for my relationships.

  That's why you must live responsibly — not just to avoid punishment but also because it's the right way to live. (Romans 13:5, MSG)

REASON # 5

A Poor Understanding of the Purpose of Marriage

I think being single may be an easier way to live

Not long ago, Tom and I were speaking to a large singles group. There was a general consensus that everyone in the group wanted to be married. It was strange, however, that when the group was casually spending time together or eating meals, most of them made negative comments and joked about marriage. They said things like, "Marriage is a lot like war, except war is easier" or "I don't know what's worse, prison or marriage." Referring to a former member of the group who had recently married, one person said, "The poor unlucky stiff went to the gallows." Sadly, the singles in this group did not even realize how negative they were about marriage.

MATT'S STORY
Matt was a thirty-eight-year-old, handsome, outgoing salesman. He and his group of friends were the "cool guys" in the group and sat in the back of the room scoping out the women. At first, they were resistant to what we had to say, cracking jokes or making defensive statements when we asked for questions.

Apparently, Matt had established a bad reputation in the group. He dated as many beautiful young women as he could, including those in the college Sunday school class, who were at least fifteen years younger than he. He quickly developed a reputation as a heartbreaker and a "player." Many eligible single women did not want to date him because they didn't want to be another addition to his list of conquests.

Later, Matt talked to us privately and said that a part of him wanted to be married, but his friends always talked about marriage in such a negative way that he was starting to wonder if it was worthwhile. He confessed that his excessive dating pattern and "confirmed bachelor" status were both ways he could cover up his deep desire to find someone to love him.

Matt had seen many of his friends get married only to divorce within a few years. They told him how lucky he was to be single and to be able to date all of these beautiful women. Even Matt's dad, who divorced his mom when Matt was twelve years old, told him that being single was an "easier" way to live. With so many married people equating marriage with confinement and constraint, Matt had trouble seeing the good in it. He is not alone.

SOCIETY'S NEGATIVE VIEW OF MARRIAGE

Jesting about marriage has been a cultural pastime for centuries, and the negativity only continues to escalate. Comedians make jokes about it and television sitcoms play up the value of the free and easy single lifestyle. Singles have consistently adopted a sarcastic tone when talking about marriage. Marriage is often seen as a demanding and burdensome endeavor that curtails one's personal freedom. Ellen Rothman encountered this pessimistic view of marriage as far back as the mid-1800s in Thomas Merrill's writings to young Daniel Webster. When

Merrill inquired if Daniel was "about to be caught in the toils of wedlock," Webster replied, "This said wedlock is a very dangerous sort of lock."[1] It seems that Matt and his buddies could have gotten some of their anti-marriage comedy routines from the critics of yesteryear.

While there was a humorous, yet apprehensive tone about marriage in the writings of the bachelors of Daniel Webster's day, men were much more responsible. Today, instead of securing land in order to make way for a family, single men are more apt to buy a new set of golf clubs or a jet ski for weekend trips with their buddies.

Many women are fearful of matrimony as well. Those who have struggled up the corporate ladder want to hang on to what they have. They buy homes, get raises, save for retirement, and wait patiently for men to make their move. Often single women have accrued wealth, property, and status equal to or greater than that of their potential suitors. This frightens them because they do not want to take care of a man financially (or emotionally, for that matter). Many singles tell us that, since marriage is not considered permanent, they worry that they may lose what they have in a messy divorce.

CHANGING ATTITUDES TOWARD THE PERMANENCE OF MARRIAGE

The sexual revolution in the 1960s ushered in the rising divorce rate of the 1970s and '80s and greatly changed society's perspective on marriage. The year 1974 marked the first time when more marriages ended in divorce than in death. Since then over half of all marriages in the United States terminate in divorce.

The implementation of no-fault divorce laws, which started in California in 1969, allowed couples to make the split without assigning blame of any kind. In a no-fault divorce, a spouse does not need to prove the other's wrongdoing, such as adultery or abuse. With the inception of this law, a spouse can file for divorce even if the other partner does not want it. The social stigma of divorce has been reduced to the point where our society views divorce as an "acceptable option." This is sad and daunting news for the millions of searching singles who want to be married but feel deeply the probability of divorce.

The ease with which our society divorces grieves the heart of God. Scripture makes clear that marriage is sacred and binding and gives very limited grounds for divorce. Matthew 5:32 says, "But I say to you that whoever divorces his wife for any reason except sexual immorality causes her to commit adultery." Today's couples have not developed the stamina to stay when times get hard. The idea of covenant marriage has faded in our society.

CHILDREN OF DIVORCE HAVE A POOR IMAGE OF MARRIAGE

The drastic increase in the divorce rate has had a profound, if not traumatic, effect on our nation's children. They are often unable to trust their partners for the security of their future marriages, especially if infidelity was involved in their parents' divorces. Divorce results in a fractured social structure because children of divorce often lose touch with at least one side of the family. The children born to parents of the "divorce gener-ation" have inherited a negative perception of marriage.

Tom and I were boomers who belonged to this divorce generation. Words like "broken home" were used to describe our circumstances and with good reason. Like the rest of this demographic group, we felt shame and a lack of social and emotional support. We were one of the many fearful couples who married in the mid-1970s with a nagging fear that our commitment might not last. We saw firsthand how hard it is to make marriage work with the looming specter of divorce hanging over your heads.

We felt that no matter how good things were, our relationship was bound to disintegrate. Along with many other adult children of divorce, we entered relationships with a sense of doom. We wrote about our struggles in our book *Adult Children of Divorced Parents: Making Your Marriage Work*.

Before we were engaged, Tom spent spring break of his first year of graduate school painting a condominium complex to earn enough money to buy a ring for me. He was a nervous wreck, and I was no better. We knew that we loved each other very much, but fear clouded our ability to trust in God and in each other for the next step. There was a mental war going on inside of us between our desire to be married and our fear that our relationship would end as our parents' marriages had.

Tom finally mustered enough courage to get down on one knee (quite a romantic gesture, which I just loved) and ask me to be his bride. You would think that I would have been elated. Part of me was, but fear reared its ugly head. My throat got scratchy, my mouth went dry, and I anxiously replied, "I don't know. Can I have a week to pray about my answer?" Can you believe I did that? How unromantic. How fearful. How sad.

Needless to say, I ruined the mood. Poor Tom put the ring back in his pocket and walked away, like a dog with his tail between his legs. I had long talks with the Lord after that, asking Him to give me a healthy, godly view of marriage. I was raised by a bitter, divorced mother who taught me to be independent so that I would never have to depend on a man. The Lord helped me see that life should be interdependent.

THE INDEPENDENT CULTURE

Society has now evolved to be a "single's culture," and independence and personal freedom are touted as the main goals in life. Today's singles climb the corporate ladder and are more independent than their ancestors. They are also loners. One study, done by a restaurant chain, showed that the vast majority of people in the Wall Street district eat their lunch alone. This is a microcosm of our society. Singles do not seem to need each other as their forebears did. In the early days of our nation, people depended on each other. Spouses counted on one another.

Innovations in our society have made it easier for us to be alone and independent, which has made marriage "unnecessary" in many ways. It has also caused our nation's young people to be ill-prepared for community. However, community is a key part of life because it helps us grow emotionally and spiritually. To Christians, community is crucial because we are mandated in Scripture to love one another.

Many of today's independent singles are self-focused and constantly looking at what they are going to get from relationships, rather than viewing them as an arena for growth. Marriage is one of the main ways that we learn to give up our self-centered natures. Michael Craven reinforces this thinking in his monograph *Why Is Marriage Important?*:

> Marriage is more profound than our contemporary culture would lead us to believe. It is a life-long commitment that restrains self-centeredness, self-indulgence, and self-gratification. It is the one relationship that effectively prepares and conditions us for community.[2]

Marriage is indeed a necessary social function and is designed to shape us and mold our independent natures into interdependence. Craven calls it the foundation for social order, and says that without it, we are headed for moral and social collapse.

Unfortunately, many of today's singles do not seem to grasp the importance of marriage. Sociologists call this the "commitment-phobic generation." While today's women may be somewhat reluctant to make a commitment, the term "commitment phobic" is typically applied to men, even in current sociological research.

WHY MEN WON'T COMMIT

Through focus groups conducted in major U.S. cities, researchers from Rutgers University interviewed single men between the ages of twenty-five and thirty-three. These men were asked to share their ideas about women, dating, and marriage. The results of the study show that men view marriage as a final step in the prolonged process of growing up. While they are young, they want freedom unencumbered by a spouse and family. Matt and his buddies echoed these findings. They told us that they did not want to marry until they got a lot of single living "out of their system."

The men in the Rutgers study also told researchers that they did not want to marry because they got plenty of sex outside of marriage. This morsel of research data even made it to Jay Leno's *Tonight Show* and received a resounding "Duh!" It seems Mr. Leno was stunned that it took research to prove what was obvious. This is a sad commentary on today's culture.

In the past, men might have dragged their feet, but there were still cultural pressures to wed. Nowadays, the traditional community and familial forces that previously encouraged single men to marry are weakened. Distance often precludes family contact and many of today's singles live in a peer world. Many have little or no contact with children. The result is a culture of men who, while they say they want to marry, delay it as long as possible. Here are the top ten reasons why single men choose to stay single according to the Rutgers study:[3]

1. They can get sex without marriage.
2. They enjoy the benefits of having a wife by cohabiting.
3. They want to avoid divorce and its financial risks.
4. They want to wait until they are older to have children.
5. They fear that marriage will require too many changes and compromises.
6. They are waiting for the perfect soul mate and she hasn't appeared yet.
7. They face fewer social pressures to marry.
8. They are reluctant to marry a woman who already has children.
9. They want to own a house before they get a wife.
10. They want to enjoy single life as long as they can.

The Rutgers study matched what Matt and the single men in his group told us. Most men do not want to commit to marriage or assume adult responsibilities. They want to stay little boys who play with their toys. This male reluctance causes women to take the lead in relationships. The trouble is, men typically do not like pushy, aggressive women. What a dilemma! Now do you see why we have the oldest and largest singles population in our nation's history?

A POSITIVE VIEW OF MARRIAGE

Our culture's notion of marriage needs an overhaul, and today's singles need to understand the true nature and purpose of marriage. The Judeo-Christian concept of marriage is as old as mankind and is the very foundation of civilization itself.

Marriage has been God's design since He created Eve for Adam. He did not want man to be alone, nor did Adam want to be. This journey of oneness was God's idea. Thomas Moore, in his great book *Soul Mates*, captures God's heart on marriage when he says,

> Without intimacy, soul goes starving, for the closeness provided by intimate relationships fulfills the soul's very nature. Family, home, and marriage each gives the soul the containment it requires. . . . Marriage is holy, not because it is a precious revered way of forming human lives, but because it is a form of religion itself, a special way in which spirituality pours into life.[4]

In his book *Mars and Venus on a Date*, John Gray gives us more of God's idea of marriage when he says,

> In spiritual terms the desire to be married is our soul remembering the sacred promise we are here to keep. It is God's will within us being felt. . . . Making marriage work is the fulfillment of one of the soul's higher purposes.[5]

Rutgers University researchers David Popenoe and Barbara Whitehead take a more practical look at marriage from a social-science perspective:

> Marriage is a fundamental social institution. It is central to the nurture and raising of children. It is the "social glue" that reliably attaches fathers to children. It contributes to the physical, emotional and economic health of men, women and children, and thus to the nation as a whole. It is also one of the most highly prized of all human relationships and a central life goal of most Americans.[6]

Dr. Linda Waite and Dr. Maggie Gallagher published their research on marriage in their groundbreaking book *A Case for Marriage*. Drs. Waite and Gallagher found that married people were happier, healthier, and better off financially than their single counterparts. These facts refute much of the conventional wisdom we hear today. When we shared these findings with Matt and his friends, they were shocked to hear that research showed marriage in such a positive light.

Contrary to what the anti-marriage culture might think, married men do not trade in their libidos for lawn mowers. One study cited by Waite and Gallagher shows that married men have more and better sex and enjoy it more emotionally and physically than single men. Single men also have a 250 percent higher mortality rate than married men. This appears to be because single men engage in particularly unhealthy, risky behaviors, such as drinking, smoking, and reckless driving. Wives typically tend to their husband's health, scheduling doctor's appointments and providing direct care. Husbands and wives also benefit from each other's emotional support during illnesses.[7]

Waite and Gallagher also found that married women are less depressed than single women. Unmarried women have a 50 percent higher mortality rate than married women. But for women, the biggest benefit by far is financial. Married women can access better housing in safer neighborhoods and have the security of owning their own homes. They are also more likely to have health insurance. Even chronically ill people who are married have a longer life span than their single counterparts.[8]

The results of Waite and Gallagher's work are overwhelming. They demonstrate that marriage is beneficial and even prove it empirically. With all of this research displaying marriage in such a positive light, it begs the question: Why do we still have singles who are afraid to commit? We believe that it is because they do not completely understand the true nature and purpose of marriage from God's perspective.

GOD'S STRATEGIC DESIGN FOR MARRIAGE

Our friend and colleague Dr. David Jenkins from Liberty University has been researching marriage from a biblical perspective for many years. He uses the term *God's strategic design for marriage* to talk about what God created men and women to do in the context of a healthy relationship. God created man in His own image. He also created all the animals of the sea, the air, and the field and gave man dominion over these (see Genesis 1:26-28). Man was responsible for tending the earth, for caring for all of creation, and for protecting all God had given him. This first man did not have the option of being passive or fearful. He was created with responsibilities and the innate abilities to meet those responsibilities.

In Genesis 2:19, we see that God brought the beasts of the field and the birds of the air to Adam "to see what he would call them." In the Old Testament, the ritual of naming was symbolic of the person or creature's nature, purpose, character, and function. In order to name these living things, Adam had to get to know them. He spent his first days on the earth establishing *relationships* with the creatures God had made.

Can't you just see this man getting to know the nature and function of every creature in order to name it? What a delight for him to know all the creatures that God had created. Genesis 2:20 says, "So Adam gave names to all cattle, to the birds of the air, and to every beast of the field. But for Adam there was not found a helper comparable to him."

Adam had relationships with all living things, but there was no one for him. He saw that the bear had a mate, the bull had a mate, even the long-necked giraffe had a mate, but there was no one like him. He was lonely, in need of a special relationship that he could call his own. In all of the creation narrative, the only thing that God said was "not good" was that man was alone (2:18). God knew Adam needed a "helper comparable," one just like him with whom he could establish a *relationship*.

This realization has caused us as marriage counselors to ask, "Do you mean the first man was hungry for relationship? Is it possible that man was the one who wanted someone with whom to connect?" This was hard for us to fathom because in our counseling offices and at our retreats, men often resist relationship. Think about it. In relationships, who is the one who typically wants connection? Who is the one who typically desires conversation? Who is often the one who asks for the define-the-relationship talks? The answer to all of these questions: the woman.

Men spend a great deal of time trying to avoid developing relationships. At home, they grab the remote, get buried in the paper, or dive into work to avoid making a connection. Even in counseling, men regularly tell us that they are just not good at "that relationship stuff." Oh, how far away man has moved from God's beautiful design.

GOD WANTS MEN TO SEE THEIR NEED

God could have made Eve at the same time as Adam, but He didn't. He wanted Adam to see his need. He wanted man to see the value of a "helper comparable." Like Matt and his male friends, today's man sees this need as negative and does what he can to put off finding a mate for as long as possible. This was not the case with Adam. He craved connection. The first man was lonely, hungry for companionship, and pining for a relationship. The loving God who put him in the garden granted his heart's desire. Adam was delighted and said,

This is now bone of my bones
And flesh of my flesh;
She shall be called Woman,
Because she was taken out of Man. (Genesis 2:23)

What is Adam doing here? He is *naming* his partner. Remember, in order to name something or someone, you have to know its character, nature, purpose, and function. You establish a *relationship* with it. Adam did this because *he* was the one who needed relationship. God designed man to be the leader. It is no wonder the women in our focus groups and counseling sessions plead for men to pursue them. It is the way God intended it to be. This is God's awesome strategic design. This is the plan we taught Matt and all of his disillusioned buddies at the singles retreat.

MATT'S HEALING

Matt began to learn about marriage from God's perspective and wanted to stop his unhealthy, shallow dating pattern. He spent time alone to learn more about who he was and who the Lord wanted him to be. During his period of soul searching, Matt began to understand that marriage was designed by God to grow you, not necessarily to make you happy and content. However, this growth can provide a great deal of happiness and contentment as you become the person the Lord has designed you to be.

When Matt decided to go back to dating, it seemed that none of the women in his church wanted to date him because of his reputation. He made a brave move and tried an online Christian dating service, where he met quite a few women who were "matches" for him and a select few he wanted to date.

After about three months of e-mailing, he finally met with

Amy, a beautiful real estate saleswoman. She was a Christian, loved kids, enjoyed the outdoors, and was only a year younger. (By this point, Matt had decided to stop dating college women because, while they were beautiful to look at, he had nothing in common with them.) He and Amy had a lot in common. They wisely took their relationship slowly and became friends first. They were committed to having a morally pure relationship and decided to practice intentional dating. Apparently, this was new for both of them, but they did not want to do anything to ruin the relationship the Lord had given them.

Matt told Amy about his extensive dating history and how he had recently gained a new perspective on marriage. She confessed that she too was disillusioned about marriage. She had virtually given up on dating, but a friend bought her a membership to the online dating service for her thirty-seventh birthday. After a year of getting to know each other, Matt and Amy were married at a beautiful wedding ceremony on the Carolina coast.

Matt and Amy told us that discovering God's strategic design for marriage was one of the best things that had ever happened to them. They both could see why marriage was good for them. Amy said it rubbed off their rough edges and taught them the give-and-take aspect of relationships, which they both desperately needed to learn.

Matt said he was glad to have someone to journey with through life's ups and downs. He told us,

Marriage has grown me in ways that I never thought possible. I am a better person and a better Christian because of my marriage to Amy. I love her more deeply than I ever thought I could. She means so much to me that I can't imagine life without her. It's not that marriage doesn't have its trials. It's just that you have someone to go through those trials with you, someone who knows you and loves you anyway, like Jesus does. It is like having a form of Christ here on earth.

Matt and Amy live close by, and occasionally we see them at the mall pushing their strollers. It seems that they were busy after the wedding. In their first three years of marriage, they had two adorable little boys, just thirteen months apart. How's that for blessings!

MAKING IT PRACTICAL: WHAT ABOUT ME?

Does your concept of the nature and purpose of marriage need an overhaul? Pray that the Lord will give you His perspective on marriage. Trust Him to do it, and He will.

FOR FURTHER THOUGHT

1. Do you ever make negative comments or joke about marriage? Why do you think you do this?

2. What have you believed about the purpose of marriage? Does your perspective align with Scripture?

3. Has your perspective about the purpose of marriage changed after reading this chapter? Has it helped you uncover any unhealthy views?

GROWING YOUR FAITH

- God created humans for relationship; therefore, my desire for a spouse is normal.

  [Jesus] answered, "Haven't you read in your Bible that the Creator originally made man and woman for each other, male and female? And because of this, a man leaves his father and mother and is firmly bonded to his wife, becoming one flesh." (Matthew 19:4-5, MSG)

- We are designed to live interdependent lives. My need for others is not a weakness.

I thank God through Jesus for every one of you. That's first. People everywhere keep telling me about your lives of faith, and every time I hear them, I thank him. And God, whom I so love to worship and serve by spreading the good news of his Son — the Message! — knows that every time I think of you in my prayers, which is practically all the time, I ask him to clear the way for me to come and see you. (Romans 1:8-10, MSG)

- Community is a crucial part of my life because it will help me to grow emotionally and spiritually.

   There are diversities in gifts, but the same Spirit. . . . But the manifestation of the Spirit is given to each one for the profit of all. (1 Corinthians 12:4,7)

Fear of Getting Hurt

I don't want to be hurt again

Patti was a thirty-nine-year-old schoolteacher and volley-ball coach who came into our office because she was disillusioned about the possibility of ever getting married. She said that she was a good woman, attended church regularly, followed the Ten Commandments, and lived a righteous life. She had been the only girl in her sorority in college who was committed to purity, and she was proud of the fact that she was still a virgin. She had worked hard to save herself for the one that God had for her, but she was single and alone.

The pain of not having a husband went deep. Patti felt she had done everything right before God, yet He had not provided her a soul mate. She watched as women who had not lived so righteously found husbands, while she remained empty-handed. "If I have to attend one more wedding of a girl in my church group who I know did not live according to Scripture, I'll scream!" Patti lamented. "This just feels so unfair to me. I feel like I try so hard with no reward."

This sense of unfairness had caused Patti to give up on love, even to stop socializing. All of her friends were married. She did not want to intrude on them, so she spent the majority of her time at work or with the children's ministry at her church. She said that if she never had the chance to have kids, at least she could be around them as much as possible.

It had been three years since Patti had been on a date. When questioned about this, she said that her last breakup had crushed her. She had been so brokenhearted and depressed that she had actually had suicidal thoughts. Her doctor had prescribed antidepressants, which she was still taking. Patti was too afraid to risk being hurt that badly again, so she consciously and unconsciously shut down with men.

Although Patti had an acute longing to be married, she was doing nothing to make it happen. She said, "I refuse to go to singles groups; I don't go to social clubs; I don't do blind dates; and I tell my friends not to fix me up with their guy friends." We hear this all too frequently from people who desperately want to find a mate but single-handedly prevent this from happening. We asked Patti how she expected to get married if she did not even put herself in situations where she could meet men. Her answer was, "If God wants it to happen, then He will just make it happen."

GOD IS NOT A GENIE

Patti was treating God like a magic genie. This is a common, but immature, perspective held by many Christian singles who want God to make things happen with little or no effort on their part. They bank on His omnipotence and don't see that they need to play an active role in achieving their goals. It's kind of like wanting to be a pianist without ever taking lessons or expecting the perfect employer to knock on their door and offer them their dream job, just because "if God wants it to happen, then He will just make it happen." It is just as unrealistic to expect God to have your future soul mate simply ring your doorbell one day and ask you to marry him or her as it is to assume that you do not have to have training or show interest to get a job. More importantly, this immature perspective can cause you to miss some valuable life lessons that God wants to teach you. Patti thought she was faithfully waiting on God, but she was actually attempting to avoid pain.

The fear of being hurt again paralyzed her. She felt that she could not take another breakup or bear to be abandoned again by another man. This pushed her into "dating withdrawal." She was so afraid to date that she sent out a "no date" signal. Everyone sends out signals or "vibes" whether he or she is conscious of it or not. You can have good vibes and draw people to you like a magnet, or you can have bad vibes, like Patti, and push people away. Patti was hypersensitive to the possibility of rejection, which made her shut down with men and have an "I'll-reject-you-before-you-reject-me" attitude.

ADAPTATION TO FEAR

Most people simply adapt to fear rather than confronting it and allowing the Lord to heal them. Their corresponding behaviors reinforce their fears rather than resolve them. By boycotting the singles scene, Patti was not demonstrating trust in God or surrender to what He wanted to do in her life. She was adapting to her fear, which only served to reinforce her wounds. The more she isolated herself from men, the more unworthy she felt. The more unworthy she felt, the more she withdrew. And so the cycle of fear goes. In order to get Patti out of this unhealthy pattern, we had to help her recognize her fear. True to the Soul Healing Love Model, we started with her family history.

PATTI'S FAMILY HISTORY

Patti was the middle of her three siblings. She described her childhood as normal; her dad worked and her mom stayed home. They were average people who cared for their children, went to church, voted, and paid their taxes. She did not report any of the typical problems that many of our clients experience. There was no divorce, death, frequent moves, or abuse that would cause severe soul wounds in her family of origin.

But when Patti was in junior high, her mother entered menopause and became irritable and depressed. Things began to slide in her house. She and her mom seemed to fight all of the time. They fought about what Patti was doing, what she was wearing, and her desire for freedom. Patti said that there was no need for her mom to be concerned. She was a good student, went to church youth group, and hung out with the smart crowd who did not get into trouble. Still, her mom was overprotective and critical.

Patti's mom also accused her of sassing and being rebellious when Patti felt like she was simply expressing her opinion and asserting her independence as a teenager. Her dad was oblivious to Patti's struggles with her mom, as his one-martini evenings turned into two or three. Looking back, she realized that her dad increased his drinking to deal with her mom's depression and the tension in the home. Her parents never resolved conflict but swept it all under the rug. Patti told herself that she would never have a marriage like theirs.

During junior high, Patti gained weight, as many adolescent girls do. She was teased by her peers and wasn't picked for teams at school or asked to school dances. She wanted to tell her parents how lonely, rejected, and hurt she felt but thought they had enough problems of their own. She then adapted to this hurt and rejection by keeping to herself. When her girlfriends developed crushes and had boyfriends, she convinced herself that she was just fine on her own.

Patti became independent, driven, and controlling—characteristics that manifested in too much self-control. She started dieting to lose weight in high school and got carried away. She struggled with eating too little and exercising too much. Now she was thin and fit, but guys still didn't ask her out.

In therapy, she realized that some of her self-control was good. After all, she was a great employee, exercised regularly, ate well, and, unlike her father, stayed away from alcohol. However, much of her controlling behavior was damaging. She was self-critical and never affirmed herself. Her extreme self-control in the area of eating and exercise was often self-punishing.

Patti's controlling behavior extended to relationships with men. She picked weaker men and tried to fix them by manipulating and lecturing. This typically caused the men to leave the relationship. Her attempts to prevent herself from getting hurt were ensuring further pain and standing in the way of finding a soul mate. She was so controlling that she could not surrender her will to the will of God.

FEAR BREEDS CONTROL

Many singles adapt to fear by being controlling. If you fear you will not find a soul mate, you will try to control the process. You will become inflexible, immovable, and want your own agenda rather than the Lord's. You may say that you wish some man would just come along and sweep you off your feet. My response is, "How can God send you a man to sweep you off your feet if your feet are glued to the floor?" Like Patti, you may be "unsweepable."

Control can cause you to have too many restrictions about your future mate. Patti would not marry a man who had been married before. She would not marry a man who had children. She would not move from her hometown. She would not go to

102 ■ The Singlehood Phenomenon

the mission field. The list of "would nots" went on and on. This did not sound like surrender to us. It sounded like control as an adaptation to her fear and a way of dealing with her pain.

We repeatedly tell singles that you cannot ask God to move and then tell Him how to do it. You have to relinquish, to abandon, to surrender your plans to Him. It soon became clear to Patti that while she claimed she had surrendered her dating to the Lord, she truly had not. Messages of fear were standing in her way.

THE MESSAGES OF FEAR

Every fear has a message that the Enemy of our souls wants us to believe. The messages of fear are "I am unworthy," "I am inferior or inadequate," and finally, "Bad things are bound to happen to me." Because so many fears are learned in the early developmental stages of life, most people internalize these messages over time. They are unable to challenge those fears realistically so resign themselves to lives of coping, rather than healing.

Patti realized that she believed all of these messages. Consciously, she thought she was practicing faith in God's omnipotent power to have her soul mate show up and sweep her away. Unconsciously, however, she felt unworthy and inadequate and feared that she would end up alone. We have found that the more you believe these messages internally, the more your fear is reinforced. You even say and do things that reinforce your fears.

The message that Patti internalized as a result of her fear was, "Men rejected me in the past because I was unworthy and inadequate, and they will reject me in the future." This internal belief was damaging her soul. Unfortunately, she dealt with her fear and its messages by trying harder, striving for more righteousness, and living above reproach. All of these efforts are good, but her striving was in her own strength and she did not trust the Lord. It also kept her locked in a cycle of fear.

The more she performed, the more defensive she became toward the Lord. She lamented to God about how righteous she was and how deserving she was of His blessing. The problem with this defensive posture is that it can cause you to wallow in unfairness and whine about injustice and inequity so much that you miss the lesson that the Lord has for you. It also prevents you from dealing with your fear.

FEAR: A POWERFUL MOTIVATOR

Fear is a powerful force in the psyche. It can control the way we think and what we do. We see this all too often with godly, righteous, singles. They are working hard to serve the Lord and do what is right in His sight, especially when it comes to dating and mating, but their fear sabotages their efforts.

Psychologists have said for years that fear is such a powerful motivator that it can consume people. Because of this, people can make their fears become reality. Proverbs 23:7 says, "For as he thinks in his heart, so is he." Fear can become the essence of who you are. In fact, your greatest fear can happen because you usher it into being.

In psychological terms this is called a *self-fulfilling prophecy*. A self-fulfilling prophecy is one in which you are so concerned about something happening that you actually make it happen, consciously or unconsciously. Patti projected her fear of being hurt onto men and ultimately onto the Lord. She was actually ushering in her worst fear.

When she was confronted about her fear, she would become defensive and offer a litany of righteous deeds she had done, and why she was deserving of blessing. She covered her fear with pride.

COVERING FEAR WITH PRIDE

There was no doubt that Patti lived a pure life. But Patti may have been doing the right things for the wrong reasons. She was a godly, well-intentioned single who tried hard to win God's favor so that she could receive the prize — a soul mate. This righteous living is wonderful, but the pride that results is not.

Patti's prayers for a soul mate consisted of sharing her spiritual résumé of good deeds with the Lord. She lamented to God about how unspiritual various engaged members of her singles group were. She told the Lord how undeserving they were of marriage, and how cheated she felt. Her judgmental attitude was laced with pride, but she could not see it. She was blinded by her fear.

The Scripture has much to say about pride and fear. The Living Bible says, "Pride disgusts the Lord" (Proverbs 16:5). Thirteen verses later, it states, "Pride goes before destruction and haughtiness before a fall" (16:18). God wanted Patti to acknowledge her pride. Rather than striving to be good enough, she needed to trust God to help her with her sin. She needed to confess her fear and pride and repent. In this way, the Lord could help her heal, take away her spirit of fear, and replace it with a spirit "of power and of love and of a sound mind" (2 Timothy 1:7).

God is in control. He is God and we are not. The Lord wants all of us to see how small we are and how big He is. God's heart is not to make us suffer, but to make us see. Not to make us hurt, but to help us heal. Performance does not earn God's gifts. Control cannot maneuver God's powerful hand.

PATTI'S HEALING

Patti told us that when she was in college she prayed for a husband. She believed that God had a plan for her to marry.

But as time progressed and this did not happen, she grew weary. She became afraid. This fear made her vulnerable to the attacks of the Enemy.

While Patti remained a servant of the Lord, in her heart she was afraid of being hurt again. This caused her to become angry with God and stop praying for a soul mate. She started living as if she would never find one, and she insulated herself with pride, determined to be sufficient on her own. This caused her not only to be closed off to men but also to quit seeking the Lord regarding His plans for her future. God seemed distant just as her earthly father had been. She could relate to the Old Testament patriarch Job as he pleaded with God, "I travel East looking for him — I find no one; then West, but not a trace; I go North, but he's hidden his tracks; then South, but not even a glimpse" (Job 23:8-9, MSG).

Job's tears and supplications were reflected in Patti's heart. Rick Warren, in his great book *The Purpose-Driven Life*, speaks of God's silence in the midst of trials when he asks, "How do you keep your eyes on Jesus when they are full of tears?"[1] Patti could relate. Warren says that often God is distant from us to test our faith. It is to help us trust Him, even when we do not feel Him or see any evidence of His work in our lives. God does this to grow us as Christians.

Warren says that when we are baby Christians, God gives us a lot of confirming emotions and often answers the most immature, self-centered prayers so that we will know He exists. But as we grow in faith, He will wean us of these dependencies. God wants us to trust Him more than feel Him. His distance can grow us. Our circumstances do not change God's character. He is still for us, even when we cannot see it.

With our help, Patti began to trust God for her future soul mate. She prayed daily for the Lord to take away her fear of being hurt and to give her the desire of her heart. Now that her faith was growing, we gave her several homework assignments to put her faith into practice.

PUTTING FAITH INTO ACTION

Faith is not faith until it has feet. Merely believing and not putting your faith into action will not help you achieve your divine destiny. One of the first assignments we gave Patti was to start attending a singles group in her local church. "What?" she exclaimed. "I hate singles groups. I stopped attending them years ago. They are like meat markets or cattle calls. This would be torture for me." We explained to Patti that this would indeed be a test of her faith, but it was also practical. If she were going to believe she had a mate somewhere, it would be wise and practical to be where single Christian men were.

Patti, as an act of blind faith, attended her first singles group function in years. She was nervous, but prayed that the Lord would help her deal with her "no date" rule and take away her feelings of unworthiness, her fear of rejection, and the prideful covering that surrounded it.

Most of the people Patti met in the group were open, warm, and friendly. This helped her get over her shyness and fear. She made a conscious effort to talk to everyone—particularly the men. In the past, her fear of rejection would have caused her to withdraw into a prideful shell. She would have appeared aloof, and no one would have approached her. She would have left the function feeling miserable and dejected, and later criticized the members of the group for being rude and shallow.

As part of the group, Patti participated in activities that she typically would not have tried before, such as hiking and tennis. She really enjoyed herself, but more importantly, her fear began to subside. We could tell that she was healing because she set a brave goal to talk to every man in the group, even if she did not think he was a potential soul mate. This was new behavior for her. Typically, if she was not romantically interested in a man she would not even talk to him. Another goal was to be especially open and warm to newcomers because she wanted them to feel welcome. She knew firsthand how hard it was for shy singles to break into a new group.

Patti befriended a newcomer named Tony and made him feel comfortable. They became fast friends and did many things together. It was wonderful for Patti to have a social life again. She particularly enjoyed the company of men, because they gave her a renewed sense of her future. It wasn't long before Tony brought his friend Gary to the group. Tony introduced Patti to Gary because he knew that she would make him feel welcome.

Tony was right. Not only did Gary feel welcomed but he and Patti hit it off immediately. He loved her warm, friendly personality. Thank goodness she was no longer hiding it. They dated for a year and a half, then Gary proposed. They felt that the Lord had saved them for each other and that they were truly blessed to have found one another. Patti assured us that had she not dealt with her fear of being hurt, she would still be participating in the self-fulfilling prophecies that had previously kept her from finding love.

MAKING IT PRACTICAL: WHAT ABOUT ME?

Have you been hurt in a love relationship? Has that caused you to fear being hurt again? Perhaps you are allowing this fear to become a reality. We have found that if singles give up their fear and stop allowing it to direct their behavior, the Lord will lead them to become their true selves. Ask the Lord to help you see your fear and surrender it to Him. Trust Him to do it, and He will.

FOR FURTHER THOUGHT

1. Are you scared to date because you are afraid of being hurt?

2. Do you think it's possible that you are living a self-fulfilling prophecy in your dating and mating? How can you overcome this?

3. Have you ever experienced pride in your dating life?

GROWING YOUR FAITH

- I can trust God to heal my hurts and give me the courage to believe that He has someone for me.

    Not that we are sufficient of ourselves . . . but our sufficiency is from God. (2 Corinthians 3:5)

- I will be more flexible and less controlling in my quest for a soul mate.

> Humble yourselves in the sight of the Lord, and He will lift
> you up. (James 4:10)

- I will examine my heart for pride in the area of dating and
mating and surrender it to the Lord daily.

> Pride goes before destruction. (Proverbs 16:18)

Wanting the Perfect Mate

I'm not a perfectionist; I'm just picky

Jared was a thirty-eight-year-old, bright, attractive banker who had quickly risen up the ranks in his company. He was basking in the American Dream with his brand-new BMW and spacious townhome in a ritzy neighborhood, fully furnished with all the toys and gadgets that a young Gen Xer could want. He was a recognized community servant, a budding political leader, and a deacon in his local church. Jared was an outgoing person with lots of friends. He was constantly on the go, traveling to exciting places, taking expensive vacations, and planning weekend getaways with his buddies.

Jared dated a lot and had fallen in love many times, but his relationships never lasted. Eventually, he found something wrong with every woman he dated. If she was pretty, she was not intellectually stimulating. If she was smart, she was boring. If she was a really good Christian, she was never fun. The summer before he came to counseling, Jared had gone on a whopping ten blind dates. That was almost one a week! He dubbed himself the "professional blind-dater," yet with all of the women he dated, he could not find a love that would last.

After spending some time in counseling, he learned that he

was what we call a *perfectionist dater.* This is a term we coined to describe a person who sets unrealistic goals about love. Jared thought if the woman wasn't a "perfect ten" in his book and he did not have tons of physical attraction and chemistry, the relationship was doomed to fail. He believed that when you meet "the one," bells will ring and whistles will blow. He was still waiting. Like many other singles, he had been victimized by our culture and its unhealthy notions of love. He believed that his feelings about a woman had to be "off the charts" before he could move toward marriage.

Jared's standards were so high that no one could live up to them. The list of things that he wanted in a woman read like a *Who's Who* in business and society. He wanted a woman with Jennifer Aniston's body, Julia Robert's smile, and Mother Teresa's heart. He also wanted her to be humble, make good money, and be a devoted Christian. She had to be fun but not wild. Happy but not ditzy. Spiritual but not judgmental. If this sounds unrealistic, it is!

This desire for powerful attraction to the perfect woman left no room for spontaneity and faith, no room for God to guide Jared's life, and certainly no room for him to be healthy in his mate-selection process. In order to find lasting love, Jared needed to discover what healthy love is all about.

PERFECTIONIST DATERS

Over the years we have treated a lot of perfectionist daters, like Jared, who have the erroneous notion that they can find "the perfect mate." It is difficult for them to make a decision about a prospective partner because they fear that someone better or more perfect may come along. As a result of this internal struggle, they place too much importance on feelings and emotions and are never satisfied in their dating relationships.

It is typical for perfectionist daters to find a great woman or man and try to "perfect" him or her even more. They may suggest that a prospective partner try some type of self-improvement such as getting an advanced degree or liposuction. Jared actually suggested to one of his girlfriends that she take elocution lessons, because he didn't like the sound of her voice. She promptly broke up with him, telling him that he was too picky. Amazingly, Jared was shocked at her response.

Perfectionist daters are formed by our society. Our culture has handicapped searching singles by selling them a notion about romantic love that is unrealistic. This societal programming causes perfectionist daters to set their standards so high that no one can live up to them. Let's face it, we have a society that eats, breathes, and sleeps sex. Advertisers sell toothpaste and chewing gum with sexy couples erotically kissing. Our culture is crazy about love, but it teaches us that love is steamy, sizzling passion that happens to only the "beautiful people."

Television sitcoms with gorgeous gals and hunky guys provide further fuel to perfectionist dating. Reality television sells romance on shows where the handsome hunk gets to pick from a bevy of perfect beauties. This does a great disservice to our nation's singles and sets them up for disappointment. When their prospective partners prove to have flaws, they are disheartened.

There is much more to mate selection than looks and chemistry. However, we are not saying that chemistry is not important. Neil Clark Warren, author of *Finding the Love of Your Life* and founder of the eHarmony online dating service, says that some physical attraction and chemistry is necessary for love to flourish.[1] While this is true, most of today's singles put entirely too much emphasis on these aspects of the relationship.

Placing too much emphasis on attraction or chemistry can be misleading because it causes singles to overlook other significant

114 ■ The Singlehood Phenomenon

aspects of mate selection, especially aspects that make a good marriage: similar values, compatibility, and common religious beliefs. You can be much healthier in the dating and mating process if you understand what happens when we "fall in love."

WHAT IS LOVE?

What is this thing called love? What is this terrible, wonderful feeling that causes us to miss sleep, lose concentration, and walk around with silly smiles on our faces? Dr. Theresa L. Crenshaw, in her book *The Alchemy of Love and Lust*, says,

> For thousands of years poets have rhapsodized about falling in love. Songs glorify it. Great thinkers have written about it. But still it retains its mystery. What magical magnet attracts us to that one special person instead of another? What happens when that electrical jolt overwhelms us? Logic and reason dissolve like smoke and we can think of nothing else. Forget concentration. Destinations don't matter. Your love becomes the atmosphere. You breathe it wherever you are.[2]

The feeling that Dr. Crenshaw identifies is actually infatuation but it is often mistaken for love by perfectionist daters.

LOVE IS NOT INFATUATION

Infatuation is what draws us to a possible partner. It is not sex drive or lust, which we will discuss later. We can have lust or sexual desire for many people, even all at once, but we can be infatuated with only one person at a time. When we become infatuated with someone, we have a heightened interest in him or her. We focus our attention toward the person, whether or not we are actually in his or her presence. Infatuation causes us to desire and to fantasize about seeing him or her again.

We daydream about that special someone and await the next meeting with bated breath. We may find ourselves playing silly love songs over and over again, because they serve as a reminder of our "new flame."

Infatuation caused Jared to have obsessive and intrusive thoughts about his newest girlfriend. As a rule, his thoughts were characteristically positive and he would assign wonderful attributes to her without really knowing her character. Herein lies the irony with infatuation. Webster properly defines it as "foolish or all-absorbing passion, lacking sound judgment . . . extrapolating from insufficient information."

When Jared first met a girl, he would form an image of who *he* wanted this woman to be. Typically, his image was far more wonderful than reality. When we're infatuated, we have an image of another person that is fantasy, not fact. This is why people say that love is blind. It is common for perfectionist daters like Jared to be swept away with infatuation because of the great emphasis they place on attraction and emotion. While infatuation can get a person into a relationship, it is not true love.

Jared's perfectionist dating also caused him to desire only women who were a "perfect ten" on the beauty scale. He said that he wanted the women he dated to be "jaw-dropping beautiful." It was hard for him to see that what he thought was love was actually physical attraction or lust.

LOVE IS NOT LUST

Lust is defined as "intense sexual desire or appetite, passionate overwhelming longing or craving." As we said earlier, one can have lust for many people all at once. It is the base mammalian part of humans, and in most mammals it is what causes them to mate. Therefore, lust is hormonally driven. Animals are literally led around by their noses. When in heat, animals emit pheromones, which attract members of the opposite sex and trigger in them the instinctive urge to mate. In some ways, Jared was acting on instinct. He would meet a beautiful woman and feel an overwhelming urge to get close to her.

The Nose Knows

Jared may have been a bit more civilized than his animal counterparts, but still, he followed their lead. Humans do not smell pheromones in the same sense that they smell food or perfume, but they do register a scent at some level of consciousness and respond to it emotionally or physically. Humans actually have a unique "smell print" that attracts members of the opposite sex.

DNA research shows that we are also attracted to people with compatible genetic composition to our own. Our body has an ability to detect someone whose DNA works best with our own in forming healthy offspring. There is a section of DNA known as HLA (human lymphocyte antigen) that functions to develop your immune system. If you mate with someone with a different or opposite HLA code, then your offspring will have greater immunity to diseases. So it is advantageous to marry someone with dissimilar DNA. Studies show that women are typically attracted to men with a dissimilar HLA coding. There is a famous study that bears witness to this.

Claus Wedekind, a noted Swiss researcher, designed a practical experiment to determine biological attraction between the sexes. He recruited forty-four men and forty-nine women as participants. The group of women was asked to smell T-shirts worn by the men and rate them according to their sexiness, pleasantness, and aversion. It seems that the women rated a man's body odor sexiest and most pleasant when his HLA profiles varied the most from their own. In other words, the women were the most attracted to the men who had a dissimilar HLA haplotype.[3]

Pheromones and DNA codings may have explained why

Jared was attracted to some women and not others. He once dated two beautiful women at the same time. His friends and family wanted him to choose the bright, responsible, level-headed banker, but he could not shake his strong attraction to a spacey, capricious, starving artist, who his parents and friends detested. It made no logical sense, but he felt more "umph" for the artist. Pheromones and DNA may be some of the reason for this inexplicable and impractical attraction. This "umph" can be far too important to perfectionist daters, like Jared. Often, they use this as the "litmus test" for love. This can be confusing, not to mention unhealthy.

Researchers say that HLA and pheromones are nature's way of progenerating or creating a healthier species. We believe that it is God at work. The Lord designed our bodies to function this way so that we could produce healthy offspring and ensure our survival. But this "umph"—what many people call chemistry—is often mistaken for love.

LOVE IS NOT CHEMISTRY

Pheromones affect dating and mating through smell, but sight can also play a part in human mate selection. Humans can see someone across the room and have a desire to get closer to him or her. Perhaps you have felt that lightning bolt that hits you the moment you spot a special someone. It causes you to see that particular person across a crowded room and do a double take. Your palms get sweaty and your heart beats fast. You long to see him or her again and again. Most people call it chemistry.

A great deal of the power of chemistry may come from the biochemical changes that occur within a person as he or she becomes infatuated. There are actually chemical changes in the brain that contribute to your feelings of well-being and euphoria. Biochemical agents in the brain work in concert to give you this "high." We have found that if perfectionist daters like Jared can learn about these brain chemicals, they are less likely to place so much emphasis on their feelings when it comes to love. Let's talk about the key players in this biochemical hormonal drama.

THE HORMONES OF LOVE

DOPAMINE

Dopamine is a neurotransmitter, which means it sends emotion-regulating signals to the brain. Its chief purpose is to give pleasure and enable us to feel joy, anticipation, excitement, and desire, including sexual desire. Because dopamine creates this desire, it plays a part in all addictive behaviors, from cocaine to sex. Dopamine is why "falling in love" can feel so intoxicating and addictive. It drove Jared to pursue each new relationship and made him obsessive when he first met a woman. Learning about this biochemical culprit helped Jared to recognize what was really happening to him.

SEROTONIN

With the advent of antidepressant drugs, we have heard a lot about this neurotransmitter. Serotonin is our well-being chemical. With high doses, we can be peaceful and serene. With lower doses, we can become irritable and depressed. However, high doses of serotonin can impede sexual desire, which is why many of the medications designed to treat depression can decrease sexual desire and function.

Serotonin regulation can be tricky when it comes to romance. If your serotonin levels are too low, you can have a great attraction to someone because your sexual drive is increasing, but this can also be accompanied by anxiety and depression. This explains why Jared was so hungry to find a woman when he was depressed. He typically would use a new woman to help him get over the depression caused by losing the previous one. This was a terribly dysfunctional pattern, because he was allowing serotonin to rule his dating life.

NOREPINEPHRINE

This neurotransmitter is best known as a treatment for asthma because it constricts blood vessels and dilates bronchi. When we "fall in love," however, it raises our blood pressure, and is associated with excitement, exhilaration, and excessive energy. This is what gives us our extra zip when we are getting to know a possible mate. Norepinephrine puts that spring in our step and allows us to go without sleep and food in pursuit of our loved one. This superhuman feeling made Jared think that each relationship must be the "real deal," only to realize much later that it had been powerful neurotransmitters operating in his body.

ESTROGEN AND TESTOSTERONE

Estrogen and testosterone are the hormones that work like polar magnets to draw men and women together. This attraction fosters various courting rituals. Researchers Givens and Perper found what they called "universal courting cues" as they observed people in singles bars. They discovered several common behaviors that men and women engage in when they are interested in each other. They found that men tend to pitch and roll their shoulders, sway from foot to foot, stand tall, or exaggerate their body movements. They may pat their hair, adjust their clothes, or tug their chins in order to attract attention from females. Women are more subtle. They smile, gaze, shift, sway, or preen. They may twist their curls, tilt their heads, giggle, raise their brows, or lick their lips in order to signal availability.[4]

These courting cues were constantly getting Jared into trouble. Whenever he met a beautiful woman who exhibited some of these movements, his hormones would take over and he was sure that he was "falling in love." True to his perfectionist dating pattern, the feeling would not last very long. He would quickly leave the relationship, wreaking havoc on the woman for whom he had declared undying love and devotion. It was helpful for him to realize the ways in which his hormones were triggered by the cues given to him by these women.

Dr. Crenshaw says that people must be careful when it comes to allowing hormones to rule them in relationships:

> Unchecked our hormones are subversive dictators with tremendous influence to sabotage our lives. Once their activity is recognized and understood, these forces can be enjoyed and/or influenced to our benefit.[5]

Perfectionist daters must be careful not to base their decisions about relationships simply on the feelings aroused by hormones.

OXYTOCIN

Oxytocin is known as the bonding chemical. High levels are found in nursing mothers, which enables them to nurture their young. It is highly activated by touch, so some call it the "cuddle chemical." Crenshaw calls oxytocin "the hormonal super glue that sticks people together."[6] Unfortunately, oxytocin also can reduce our ability to think and reason clearly, which is why love can cause you to lose concentration and to act goofy in general.

When Tom and I started dating in college, we were so frustrated at ourselves because we simply could not focus. We forgot deadlines on papers, couldn't remember when to turn in projects, and missed classes, all of which caused our grades to take a nosedive. Looking back, we can see that oxytocin was inhibiting our ability to concentrate on anything but each other. Jared shared our plight. As oxytocin would course through his veins, he would lose concentration and become "love struck," causing him to feel as though he had found true love. While this is a great feeling, it is unhealthy to think that it is love. It is a part of love, but true love is a great deal more.

PHENYLETHYLAMINE

Phenylethylamine (PEA for short) is the love drug of the millennium. It is a chemical cousin to an amphetamine so it creates a natural high. As with any amphetamine, PEA offers a great, but false, sense of well-being. It makes you feel superhuman and euphoric, and this feeling can be addictive. Levels of PEA fluctuate with your thoughts and feelings about romance or your romantic partner, which is why you can conjure up this great feeling simply by reliving a romantic scene in your mind. PEA also causes certain physical symptoms, such as heart palpitations and sweaty palms.

When Tom and I first met, we couldn't get enough of each other, or should we say, of PEA. We would go to great lengths to change our schedules just to see each other for fifteen minutes, allowing that short biochemical "hit" to last us all the next day—and it did! We'd forget to eat and sleep and would stay up to all hours talking about nothing, just to hear the sound of each other's voice. Little did we know that we were not high on love, but on phenylethylamine. Jared realized that he had fallen victim to PEA many times and confused the feelings it generated for true love.

While PEA has its good qualities, studies show that too much PEA can make you crazy. High doses have been found in schizophrenics. An abundance of PEA can trigger mania, anxiety, sleep disturbance, and psychotic behavior. So, while it is indeed wonderful, it can be destructive as well, and it certainly contributes to love's seeming insanity.

When PEA is flowing through our bodies, we tend to be

unrealistically optimistic. At the beginning of the relationship, we become delusional and frame our partners' weaknesses in the most positive light. Her temper tantrums become passion. Her tightness with money becomes responsible frugality. His obvious proclivity for drink becomes a "misunderstanding." The super-human effect of PEA makes us feel invincible. Unfortunately, seeing our partners through rose-colored, biochemical-laden glasses lasts for only a while.

As with most chemicals in the system, our bodies build up a tolerance to it. After a while it takes more and more PEA to produce love's special kick. As the chemical wanes, a more realistic image of our partners appears. As we see our partners for who they really are, we can second-guess ourselves and our partners, which often leads to disappointment.

While there are dips in one's PEA levels—first at three months, then two years—it takes about four years for PEA to run its full course. By the four-year mark, the effects of PEA and the many other brain chemicals wear off and we no longer feel love's special kick. Our partner falls off his or her pedestal and becomes a mere mortal.

Often this is when perfectionist daters become so disillusioned that they exit the relationship, repeating the cycle every four years. Social scientists call these people "serial monogamists" or "attraction junkies." Knowing that there is a natural biochemical reason for partners to fall from grace can help you decide to *love* rather than allow brain chemicals to rule you.

Jared learned that he was an attraction junkie who confused brain chemical highs with true love. He was particularly addicted to PEA and loved the feeling that accompanied a new relationship. Sadly, when the feeling began to wane, he immediately thought that the relationship was doomed. This caused him to write off several wonderful women who may have been potential soul mates.

THE FOUR-YEAR ITCH

Arriving at the four-year mark in a relationship can be hard on a couple. Tom and I loved the chemically laden high at the beginning of our relationship. I can safely say that I could have been a phenylethylamine addict. I truly enjoyed the superhuman feeling, sweaty palms and all. There was a sense of connection that our biochemical helpers brought us. Tom could be standing three aisles over in Wal-Mart and clear his throat, and it would make the hair on the back of my neck stand up. Not only would I know he was there, I would get tingly all over. We finished each other's sentences, read each other's minds, and clairvoyantly knew when the other would call. Little did we know that these feelings would take a drastic downturn within four short years.

We mistakenly thought that this feeling was love and that it would never end. When we reached the dreaded four-year point and our PEA levels were drastically waning, we were poor, childless, and struggling through the grueling demands of graduate school. This stress in our marriage came at a very inopportune time.

Suddenly my heart did not go "pitter-patter" when Tom walked in the door from school. There was no "zing" inside me that led to an automatic smile, and there was no desire to greet him with a welcoming hug and kiss. We wondered what happened. How had our relationship died so suddenly? We were terribly concerned that we had fallen out of love.

Many of our friends did not share our dilemma. When we entered graduate school, they entered parenthood. It seemed that they had children to focus on and glue them together. We, on the other hand, had to take stock of our relationship and see where it was headed. We were up to our necks in stress and fresh out of phenylethylamine.

We had many discussions about what love really was. After

many hard talks and the help of a marriage counselor, we finally realized that love is not a feeling. It is a choice that involves conscious commitment. It was at that point that we moved from unconscious attraction (brain chemicals and phenylethylamine) to a conscious choice to love each other, which is hard work.

LOVE IS A CHOICE

Love is more than a feeling. Happily ever after takes conscious effort. After almost thirty years of moves, mortgages, children, deaths, struggles, and triumphs, we rejoice that we made the choice to love each other. We learned the hard way that putting too much emphasis on feelings can leave lovers leveled when it comes to finding real love.

With all that we have discovered, we no longer use the term "falling in love" when referring to a couple smitten with each other. We now call it "tripping into infatuation" because the fall is more like a stumble, and the feeling is infatuation, not true love. True love is a decision that is made with the conscious, intentional part of the brain. In the past twenty-five years we have helped countless singles and couples find a healthy lasting love by making the same conscious choice. Jared was one of those people.

JARED'S HEALING

We taught Jared a more healthy process of mate selection. It is not that we wanted him to settle for less or end up in a relationship with an unattractive "geek" for the rest of his life. We just counseled him to be more realistic, conscious, and healthy about the women to whom he was attracted. Somewhere between pheromones, DNA, and phenylethylamine, he began to believe that something greater was happening inside of him than his quest for the "perfect woman."

As Jared began to understand what was actually happening to him when he "tripped into infatuation," he could respect his body chemistry instead of allowing it to rule him. He saw what the psalmist said was true in Psalm 139:13-14:

> For You formed my inward parts;
> You covered me in my mother's womb.
> I will praise You, for I am fearfully and wonderfully made.

Jared saw that God created a great masterpiece when He formed the human body. This helped him to understand how God intended for humans to mate. It also helped him to make a conscious choice to find a mate and to trust God in his selection. Jared became more sensible and healthy in his dating relationships and learned to set realistic standards for prospective partners.

It was not long after that when he met Marie, a warm, vivacious, compassionate social worker. Marie was a young divorcée who married while she was in college. Shortly afterward, her husband left her because he belatedly decided he wasn't ready for such a big commitment. Jared told us that if he had not done his internal work, he would not have considered Marie as a prospective partner because she was not "his type." Not only was she divorced, she was not like the "supermodels" that Jared was used to dating. Marie was not off-the-charts gorgeous, but she had an earthy, natural beauty that drew people to her. He found that there was something comforting about her smile, and her internal beauty made her glow.

At first, Jared kept his distance from Marie because he did not feel the powerful chemistry that he was so familiar with. We encouraged him to look harder, and he found that there was indeed chemistry between them. It was just different from what he had experienced before. Instead of a lustful magnetic attraction, it was more like a gentle, spiritual nudge. Jared had to fight the urge to abandon this new kind of relationship because it was unfamiliar. However, as time went on, he grew to care a great deal for Marie, as she did for him.

He stayed the course with Marie, and they developed a beautiful love for one another, like none he had ever experienced. He realized that if he had stayed on the path he had been traveling, he would probably still be a single, alone, perfectionist dater to this day. One of the happiest moments for us as counselors was to help officiate at Jared and Marie's wedding. At the beautiful wedding reception they had overlooking the mountains of North Carolina, Jared made a toast to his brand-new wife. "To Marie, who helped me stop my quest for the perfect woman and find the woman who was perfect for me."

Tom and I may have been the only guests there who really knew the power of Jared's words and how hard he worked, with the Lord's help, to overcome his unhealthy, perfectionist patterns so that he could find his soul mate. Our eyes misted with his as we watched him declare his gratitude to Marie and the Lord for the love he was experiencing.

MAKING IT PRACTICAL: WHAT ABOUT ME?

What about you? Are you a perfectionist dater looking for the "perfect person?" Maybe it is time to ask the Lord to pick a mate for you, rather than allowing your biochemistry to rule you. Pray that the Lord will help you get a realistic look at your dating style and make it healthy. Trust Him to do it, and He will.

FOR FURTHER THOUGHT

1. Have you ever dated someone that you tried to perfect or who tried to perfect you? How did it affect the relationship?

2. How much weight do you place on attraction when deciding whom to date? Has it ever caused you to overlook someone who may have been perfect for you?

3. Have you ever confused brain chemicals with true love?

GROWING YOUR FAITH

- Understanding how my body is designed can help me make wiser choices in my dating life.

    I will praise You, for I am fearfully and wonderfully made.
    (Psalm 139:14)

- We are all made in the image of God. It's not my job to improve someone else or respond to his or her attempts to improve me.

So God created man in His own image; the image of God
He created him; male and female He created them. (Genesis
1:27)

- Love is a choice and making that choice takes hard work,
but God will help me do this work.

Therefore a man shall leave his father and mother and be
joined to his wife, and they shall become one flesh. (Genesis
2:24)

Not Dealing with Prior Heartbreak

I don't want to feel the pain

Todd called to ask for our advice about some difficult dynamics in the thriving local singles group he pastored. His group had quite a few singles who had been married before and many of them were dating very shortly after they were separated. In North Carolina, couples have to wait one year after filing for divorce before it is final. This means that the singles in Todd's group were dating while they were still legally married. This is not only unhealthy but also unbiblical. Todd had preached many sermons about this, but the members of the group were not heeding his advice.

North Carolina is not alone in establishing this one-year-waiting-period law. Many states have adopted this waiting period to give couples time to think through their decision and avoid rushing into a divorce or into another relationship. Studies show that states that have this waiting period have a higher rate of reconciliation than those that do not.

Lawmakers established this law based on the information and opinions of professional counselors who have studied the length of the grieving and healing period after the dissolution of a marriage. As a rule, it takes about one year for every four that you were married to grieve for the loss and recover. So if you were married for four years, waiting at least a year before dating is a smart thing to do. People who are dating within a year after their separation may not have fully grieved their loss and have a high risk of being in a rebound situation. Not only is this harmful for the separated person but it can also be risky for the unlucky person who gets picked as the "significant other."

These in-between relationships (those that occur between marriages) have been dubbed *transitional relationships*. Typically they do not last because people do not take the time to sort out what went wrong in their last relationship. They haven't had time to recover from the loss. If they do not grieve properly, they are prone to rebound and repeat the same dysfunctional patterns all over again.

PAIN CAN PRODUCE GROWTH

Most of us do not want to take time to grieve because it is too painful. We want to find someone to love us, care for us, and take the pain away as quickly as possible. A period of separation is painful and lonely, but this time can help you to grieve and heal.

Mark McMinn, in his book *Psychology, Theology, and Spirituality in Christian Counseling*, speaks to Christian counselors about the purpose of pain when he says,

> Discomfort often motivates insight, and when we use clinical tricks to erase misery prematurely from our clients' lives, we short-circuit their opportunities for emotional and spiritual growth. Throughout Scripture and throughout the history of the Christian church, God has used pain to bring people to maturity.[1]

Many of the people in Pastor Todd's singles group were not grieving. There were several newly separated men and women who were making the rounds. One couple, Bill and Stacy, had been dating six months and were already talking about marriage. They had been separated from their spouses for only a short while, so neither of their divorces were final. Pastor Todd and other members of the group were concerned that they were both rebounding and using each other as a distraction to buffer the pain and rejection of their respective separations.

Pastor Todd sensed that both Bill's and Stacy's wounds were still fresh, because any time they mentioned their marriages, they were angry, resentful, and bitter. Neither of them would take any blame or responsibility for what had happened in their past breakups, and they blamed the collapse of their respective marriages solely on their partners. It seemed that discussing their marital wounds was one of the main things they had in common. Their feelings of victimization toward their estranged spouses formed an unhealthy bond between them.

Many of you have been in dating relationships like this, where someone spends most of his or her time telling you about the evil ex-partner, as if the past wounds were still new. This is not only a turnoff but also a sure sign that the person has not recovered from his or her previous breakup.

Bill's and Stacy's unresolved grief kept their wounds fresh and fed their resentment, bitterness, and unforgiveness. They had a great deal of fear that they were going to be reinjured, especially by each other. They were hypersensitive to almost everything the other did, especially if it came close to replicating patterns that occurred in their previous marriages. This hypersensitivity was killing their relationship, and they did not even know it. Bill and Stacy blamed the struggles in their relationship on each other, in the same way they blamed all of the problems in their previous marriages on their spouses.

This happens frequently with people who have not properly recovered from past relationship breakups. Bill and Stacy were injuring each other in ways similar to those in which their not-yet-ex-spouses injured them. They tried hard not to step on each other's soul wounds, but they just couldn't help it. Their own wounds were open and oozing.

Any time Bill did anything that would remotely resemble a negative act committed by Stacy's former husband, she would overreact and become hysterical. She would then panic and threaten to break up with Bill. Stacy was so afraid of being trapped in another miserable relationship that she was constantly on guard and would react too emotionally to Bill's slightest action.

STACY'S AND BILL'S REACTIVITY

Stacy and Bill had a great deal of reactivity toward each other. Bill's ex-wife had had an affair with one of his friends, which devastated him. Stacy had many male friends in the singles group, and when she greeted them, she was warm, friendly, and funny. She would even flirt a little because she saw many of these guys as her "buddies." This made Bill insanely jealous because it reminded him of his ex-wife, whose flirtation led to an affair. He would become reactive and criticize Stacy, complaining about how she liked the attention of men and was shallow and untrustworthy. At times he even accused her of having loose morals.

This criticism devastated Stacy because she felt that what Bill said was unfounded. It also triggered a wound in her from her ex-husband, who was highly critical. She would get very reactive with Bill and threaten to break up with him. Bill would feel manipulated and call her bluff by telling her to go ahead and leave. In the six months that they dated, they had broken up four times! Their attraction, connection, and chemistry made it difficult for them to stay apart, so within a few days they would get back together, only to repeat the cycle again.

After four traumatic breakups, Bill decided not to go back to Stacy. Within a week, he started dating Natalie, a pretty young woman who was new to the group. This did not sit well with Stacy and all of her friends. They were angry with Bill and snubbed him and Natalie at church and at other singles venues, which was not a charitable or Christlike reception for a newcomer. Stacy quickly had a friend fix her up with yet another guy in the group to make Bill jealous. It worked, and they both promptly dumped their transitional people to pursue each other yet again. This created two more innocent victims in their childish love quadrangle. These crazy dating relationships hurt so many people in the group that it prompted Pastor Todd to call us.

"What a mess!" he said. "These people have not finished their first marriages, much less their 'transitional relationships,' and now they are wreaking havoc on the remaining singles in my group." Todd asked us to come and do a Soul Healers Singles Retreat with his group and perhaps spend some time counseling some of his group members. During the weekend, we gave the members a chance to sign up for counseling. At the top of the list was Stacy, followed by Bill.

STACY'S STORY

As we sat down with Stacy, there were tears in her eyes as she talked about how painful her marriage and separation had been and how critical her ex-husband was of her. She also shared how Bill was very much like him. According to Imago relationship theory, if you do not become consciously aware of your unhealthy attraction patterns, you may be destined to pick mates who are similar to each other. Therefore, if you have a bad relationship and do not properly recover from it, you have a great likelihood of picking someone very similar to your ex-partner and repeating the same unhealthy patterns. Stacy and Bill were doing just that.

We asked Stacy how long she waited after her separation before dating.

"Oh, a month or two," she answered.

"Why so soon?" we asked.

"Because it was so nice to have someone want me. I was lonely and felt terribly rejected and unlovable. It was great to have someone come along and take the pain away."

This is a common mistake for singles. They think that dating quickly takes away the hurt. The truth is that it masks it for only a while. It simply delays the grief that people need to experience in order to heal and recover from the breakup. Dating is often like aspirin for a headache. It masks the symptoms and numbs us from feeling pain, but it does not heal the root cause of the headache. People think that they are healing by getting back in the dating scene, but they are actually harming themselves and others. To help singles deal with this, Tom and I have developed what we call *singles group dating etiquette*.

SINGLES GROUP DATING ETIQUETTE

There is no official rulebook for singles who are dating members within their own singles group. However, because these groups can become very tightly knit, dating needs to be treated with integrity. Singles need to use common sense, be respectful of each other's feelings, and strive to be more Christlike with one another. Obviously it is not healthy, godly, or good etiquette for singles to date when they are still married. But, for those who have waited to heal from their past relationship, there are some healthy things to do.

Singles tell us that they have trouble dating in singles groups because of the lack of privacy. They do not like for others to know their business. Typically, if a couple in the group has been dating, and they break up, it can affect many people in the group. People may take sides in the breakup or make it the new "hot" topic of gossip. In light of this, it is a good idea for singles to take their time before starting to date again, especially if they are going to date someone within the singles group. A good time period is about three months.

We call this the *three-month rule*. It usually takes at least three months to sort things out, get over your hurt and anger, and grieve. If you get back into the dating scene too quickly, you are in danger of rebounding and hurting others. Both Stacy and Bill said that if they had the benefit of this information, perhaps they would not have gotten off to such a rocky start.

It is important to note that rules like waiting three months after a breakup, not dating to make your ex jealous, or getting involved in rebound relationships are true generally, not just in singles groups. Playing games and using people for your own gain is unhealthy, but more importantly, ungodly. God desires that we treat others with respect.

FEELING IS HEALING

We encouraged Bill and Stacy—as we encourage anyone who has just experienced a breakup—to feel their pain. In the Soul Healing Love Model we have a saying: "You can't heal what you can't feel." Allowing ourselves to feel the pain, hurt, and rejection of the demise of a relationship can teach us many things. Unfortunately, many people want to avoid grieving because it is so painful. We are a society that does not grieve well. In the 1970s, there was a popular song by Carly Simon called "Haven't Got Time for the Pain." This pop culture testimony to western society's tendency to avoid pain contrasts sharply with other cultures in the news. A bomb hits a mall in Jerusalem, and parents, loved ones, and even onlookers scream in horror and sorrow. They fall to the ground in pain and violently express their sadness over this tragedy. Police in droves have to hold back anguished family members who wail and throw themselves at their dead loved ones.

This type of grieving is normal, yet our culture prides itself on our calm, stoic manner. We brag about spouses who remain "dignified" at funerals, so as not to appear unseemly. We see their avoidance of grief as strength, but true strength is found in those anguished souls who have the courage to express their grief.

I still remember the funeral of President John F. Kennedy. There on the television, for all of America to see, were his beautiful wife and two small children. Jackie Kennedy was standing there, saying goodbye to her life's companion and she had to hold back tears. The nation praised her for what they perceived as strength and decorum. I thought this was so sad.

In contrast, several years later, Ethel Kennedy, the mother of eleven children, and wife of the murdered Senator Robert Kennedy, threw herself on the casket and wept openly with her sorrowful children at the televised funeral. "How inappropriate," people said. To have so much emotion in public was unrefined and almost uncouth. Why? Because it made folks feel uncomfortable. That's right. We *were* uncomfortable, because we are taught to bury our grief when we bury our dead.

I was only a child when I witnessed the funerals of these great men on television. I remember the praise my family gave Jackie Kennedy for her reserved demeanor, and the frustration they expressed toward Ethel. The thought occurred to me, even at a young age, that despite what society says, Ethel was more real! In a society that "hasn't got time for the pain," we need to go against the grain and make time to grieve. This is especially true for singles who experience the hurt and pain of a relationship breakup.

GRIEVING BRINGS ABOUT RESPONSIBILITY

Grieving can also bring about healthy guilt and responsibility. It can show us what *we* did wrong in our relationship, as well as what our partner did. Just as physical pain is an indicator that something is wrong in our body, emotional pain can show us what went wrong in our relationships. The trouble is most of us fight the healthy guilt and responsibility; we resist acknowledging the unhealthy part we play in our relationships. We are more comfortable being a victim of a cruel ex than taking responsibility for our own dysfunctional behaviors.

When people come in for counseling, whether they are married, engaged, or just dating, they can typically give us a list of their partner's flaws. However, people are seldom willing to share their own faults. It seems that it is human nature to blame others. Seeing the part you play in past or present relationship struggles can enable you to make healthy changes in the future.

We encouraged Bill and Stacy to "get real" about the part they played in ending their marriages and in damaging their relationship with each other. We asked them to pray and do some real soul searching about the past. If they had trouble becoming aware, they could just look at the issues that they were currently reacting to with each other. This would shed some light on their previous marital struggles.

STACY GETS REAL

Stacy saw that both Bill and her husband thought she was too flirtatious, which, in turn, made her feel that both of them were being excessively critical and controlling. This gridlock of opposing opinions caused strife in her marriage and in her relationship with Bill. She said that for many years she tried to deny it, but with prayerful examination, she could see their point. As she "got real," she had to admit that some of what Bill and her ex-husband were saying was true. She *did* like to flirt and wanted the attention of other men—perhaps not at the level that Bill insinuated, but nevertheless it was present.

Upon further self-examination, and with the help of some questions in counseling, Stacy saw that her need for male attention was predicated on the fact that she was the fifth of five children. Her parents seemed old and tired by the time she came along and did not have much patience with her. They were constantly criticizing her for trying to get attention or for being too sensitive, which created soul wounds for her. Stacy realized that both her ex-husband and Bill triggered these soul wounds when they criticized her.

Stacy became reactive to Bill because he criticized her flirtatious behavior. Bill was very reactive to Stacy because her flirting triggered a wound from his ex-wife, whose attention-drawing behavior led to an affair. Both of them found that they were triggering each other's fears and creating reactivity in one another. In the Soul Healing Love Model, we call this phenomenon *interactivity*.

INTERACTIVITY

Interactivity occurs when the soul wounds in one partner are triggered and his or her reactivity triggers the soul wounds in the other person, who then becomes reactive as well. This is a ready-made formula for a power struggle and is just where Bill and Stacy found themselves. We define a power struggle as "a situation in which there is an underlying tension that is characterized by fear, which results in a breakdown of communication that leads to assumptions. In the power struggle, a couple typically assumes the worst about each other."[2]

Both Bill and Stacy did exactly that. We told them that the only way out of the power struggle was to begin to understand the part that each of them played. To end a power struggle you must acknowledge your fear and negative thoughts, and stop projecting them onto your partner. You must then make a conscious choice to give up your right to react. This is what we call *intentionality*.

INTENTIONALITY

Intentionality is the ability to act in a healthy manner no matter how you feel. It is a concept used in self-help groups involving behaviors like alcoholism or drug addiction. The old adage "Fake it till you make it" comes to mind when we teach people intentionality. Alcoholics Anonymous teaches that even if you are desperate for a drink, you should walk past the bar door and act as if you do not want one. After a while, your feelings will follow your behavior.

Many AA participants refer to this as "white-knuckle sobriety." This means staying sober is an act of will and not dependent on feelings or emotions. We call intentionality in marriage "white-knuckle matrimony." You consciously choose to act in a healing manner no matter how you feel. One wonderful thing about intentionality is that you can't practice it and be reactive. At times this can be very hard, especially when certain emotions rear their ugly heads to remind us of the past.

We certainly don't want people to become fake or phony. However, sometimes we are so reactive that we become unreasonable. Intentionality is an aspect of self-control, which Galatians 5:22 tells us is a fruit of the Spirit. Self-control or intentionality enables couples to keep their cool even when their soul wounds are triggered. A cool head helps them to differentiate current relationship struggles from past traumas. As intentionality helps couples separate the present from the past, they can then grieve for the past, learn from it, and recover from the hurt.

Bill and Stacy learned how to practice intentionality, which enabled them to stop their reactivity and interactivity. Since they were not as emotionally focused on themselves, they could learn to empathize with each other.

STACY'S INTENTIONALITY

Stacy began to work on understanding how and why Bill triggered her. Rather than defending her flirtatious behavior, she saw herself through Bill's eyes. She realized that her behavior wounded him because it reminded him of what his ex-wife had done. By practicing intentionality, Stacy started to understand what Bill projected onto her. She could see herself as Bill saw her and how her behavior hurt him. She also realized that her flirtation met a need in her that was unhealthy, and certainly no longer necessary. Stacy had a good man who paid a lot of attention to her. She did not need to seek extra attention from other men.

In the past, one man's attention was not enough to counteract Stacy's negative self-image. The interesting thing was that even with all of the attention she received as a result of her flirtations, she still felt empty and unlovable. She was beginning to see that Bill's sincere, heartfelt attention, along with the Lord's unconditional love, were indeed enough to satisfy her. This was the beginning of some great insight and healing for Stacy.

HEALING YOUR PARTNER HEALS YOU

As is often the case, when Stacy made changes in her behavior to help Bill heal, she too received healing. This is soul healing—putting your pride aside and acting intentionally to overcome the soul wounds that make you wound your partner. By doing this you have the opportunity to heal. This is part of God's wonderful plan for oneness.

As a part of her healing, Stacy confessed to Bill that he was right in many ways. She had an unhealthy need to seek attention from men. Seeing how she caused Bill pain not only helped her change but also helped Bill see that she truly desired to empathize with him. Bill expressed a great deal of gratitude toward Stacy for the caring and the courage it took to share so openly.

Stacy's honesty actually healed a lot of Bill's soul wounds that were inflicted by his ex-wife. He said that his former wife could never own the part she played in being impudent in their marriage. The fact that Stacy humbly owned her part was healing for him. This also helped Bill see the unhealthy role he played in his relationships and the unresolved issues from his past that kept him imprisoned.

BILL'S HEALING

Bill was the oldest child in a family of three children. His father was a colonel in the army, with very high expectations of himself and his children, especially his oldest son. He was a critical man and often tried to motivate Bill through criticism, saying things like, "You will never get an A in that class because you are such a slacker. You need to try harder." Bill responded to his dad's negativity by performing harder to prove his dad wrong. The harder he worked to be successful, the more his fear of failure was reinforced. The dissolution of his marriage caused the term "slacker" to echo in his psyche even more.

Since Bill responded to his father's criticism by trying harder, he thought everyone would respond in the same way. Sadly, he followed his dad's example. He criticized his ex-wife in order to motivate her to change, and he also criticized Stacy. He learned after careful self-examination and prayer that his criticism caused those he loved to feel defeated and unloved.

Unfortunately, he learned this principle the hard way. The more unloved his ex-wife felt, the more she sought attention from men who could make her feel better about herself. She responded to Bill's criticism by finding someone who would not criticize, but would adore her. She eventually left Bill for this man. Seeing this showed Bill the part he played in pushing his ex-wife into a painful affair. Bill grieved over his mistakes and bravely took responsibility for the part he played.

Bill further saw that not only had this critical behavior damaged his marriage but it threatened his relationship with Stacy. So, Bill got real with himself and Stacy. Like her, he felt that he was not as critical as she alleged. He thought that she was projecting a bit, but he started to see himself through her eyes. He could see how his critical behavior had caused her pain. Bill confessed this to Stacy, which moved them toward forgiveness.

GRIEVING LEADS TO FORGIVENESS

Perhaps the most important part of grieving is that it leads to forgiveness, the ultimate recovery. It is rarely easy to forgive, especially if someone has used you and broken your heart, but theologically speaking no one deserves forgiveness. God grants it by His grace and commands that we do the same. He knows that the trap of unforgiveness will keep us captive. The offender does the crime but if you cannot forgive, you serve the sentence. As Malachy McCourt once said, "Resentment is like taking poison and waiting for the other person to die."

Unforgiveness creates an unhealthy bond with the begrudged person. It allows bitterness and hate to ferment in our souls. Think about it. The inability to forgive causes us to think of the offender often, perhaps even more than those we love. We are prone to rage, especially in romantic relationships. It seems that the closer we were to a person, the harder it is to forgive him or her. We may want to drum up support from other people against him or her and make sure everyone knows just how heinously he or she behaved. We desperately need the freedom that forgiveness brings.

FORGIVENESS IS HEALING

Let's take a look at the word *forgive*. It is actually two words together. First is the word *for*, which means "to be used in connection with." [3] Next is *give*, which means "to present voluntarily without expecting compensation, or to relinquish or sacrifice." [4] Together, it is *forgive*. It is a procedure *for giving* something that is not deserved. The paradox about forgiveness is that it is not only *for giving* pardon to the undeserving offender but also *for giving* freedom to ourselves. When we begin the process that, at first, is *for giving* to our perpetrator, that same process results in the liberation *we* so desperately need. Thus, the act of forgiveness is curative.

There is another reason why forgiveness is so important for Christians. It is the example of the sinless Christ who walked this planet and suffered great and undeserved persecution and abuse. He ultimately sacrificed His life in order to forgive our sins. Christ's example calls us to sacrificially forgive those who have caused us pain. Acting in a Christlike way and forgiving those who have broken our hearts is hard, but it has immeasurable results. Bill and Stacy bore witness to this firsthand.

A HAPPY ENDING

Bill and Stacy's journey into grieving and recovering from the loss of their past relationships was tremendously healing. They learned about their own soul wounds and saw how they were triggering each other's soul wounds. Grieving also showed them the part they played in the dissolution of their respective marriages, as well as the unhealthy part they were playing in their relationship with each other. They were able to change their behaviors and, eventually, to forgive their ex-spouses.

After dealing with the hurts from their past breakups, Bill and Stacy took some time to reflect, be alone, and grow spiritually. They waited for their divorces to be finalized and sought the Lord about what He wanted for them. They even tried to talk to their ex-spouses and ask for forgiveness for what they had done wrong. This took a great deal of strength and was very freeing for both of them.

As time passed they both felt that the Lord was leading them to get back together. Because they did not carry baggage from their previous relationships, Bill and Stacy became a strong, powerful, soul-healing couple. Two years after we met Bill and Stacy, they got married. They had grown together in such a healthy way that they were a shining example to their families and friends of what a soul-healing couple could be.

While they were engaged, they started a small group where they taught singles how to recover from past breakups and properly grieve their losses. What we taught them about recovery was so important to them that they wanted other singles to experience it as well. After all, if they had not grieved and recovered from their past breakups, their relationship would not have survived.

MAKING IT PRACTICAL: WHAT ABOUT ME?

How about you? Have you had a relationship that ended painfully? Have you fully recovered? After reading this chapter, do you believe your lack of healing is haunting you and causing you to be reactive? Pray, and ask the Lord to show you any grieving that you may need to do. Trust Him to do it, and He will.

FOR FURTHER THOUGHT

1. How do you typically grieve the end of a relationship? Do you think you give yourself enough time to recover?

2. Can you see what part you've played in relationships that have ended? Have you always been willing to acknowledge your role?

3. Is there someone you've been romantically involved with that you need to forgive?

GROWING YOUR FAITH

- Unforgiveness will keep me in chains. I will forgive because Christ forgave me.

  "For if you forgive men their trespasses, your heavenly Father will also forgive you." (Matthew 6:14)

- Although grief is painful, it can be an opportunity for emotional and spiritual growth.

> "Blessed are those who mourn,
> For they shall be comforted." (Matthew 5:4)

- Despite my past, I have the opportunity to develop healthy relationships if I am willing to look at my faults—not just someone else's.

> "Judge not, that you be not judged. . . . First remove the plank from your own eye, and then you will see clearly to remove the speck from your brother's eye." (Matthew 7:1,5)

An Unbalanced Focus on Career

I want to be established before I get married

Erica, an anesthesiologist, sought help from our counseling center because she was forty-two years old and felt she was in a rut. Her life consisted of working late at the hospital and crashing in bed at night. With the exception of church, her patients were all she had. She loved ministering to them and felt that she was doing what the Lord created her to do. Although Erica enjoyed her work, she never thought she would reach the age of forty as a single, childless woman. Because of her shy nature, making friends and establishing a social life took a lot of effort for little reward. Eventually she just quit and put her energy where she felt it was most useful—her work.

Emily had a somewhat similar situation. She was approaching her fortieth birthday, and the production company she started had gone public, making it possible for her to retire early in a very comfortable financial position. She was an over-achiever who loved her work and enjoyed having her gifts used and recognized by others. Emily took every opportunity she could to share her faith and gave credit for her success to the Lord. She felt guilty and weak for not being fulfilled by all she had, but she had always wanted to be a wife and mother. "I should be happy for all that I have," she cried. "But this is not all I wanted at age forty. I wanted to be happily married and have a family. It just seems that there was always something else to do that got in the way."

When Emily complained to her mother about wanting a husband and children, her mom minimized the importance of this and told her how lucky she was, as a woman, to have achieved such success. Emily's mom said that marriage and family were overrated and would often share the painful details of her divorce from Emily's dad. The bitterness and resentment in her mom's voice were obvious as she complained that she never achieved her career goals, because she was a divorced woman with children. "Stick to your career goals," her mom would say. "You are doing something that men will never be able to take away from you." This left Emily feeling grateful yet, at the same time, perplexed and alone.

There are many women today like Erica and Emily who are successful, overachieving, career oriented, and single. They are using their gifts for the Lord and doing a great job of it. The trouble is they are doing such a good job that they have little room for anything else. These women wanted a husband and a family but were too busy with their careers.

Sylvia Ann Hewlett, author of *Creating a Life: Professional Women and the Quest for Children*, says that many women who have pursued successful careers, accumulated status, and achieved comfortable incomes are feeling the angst of child-lessness. She states that legions of successful women from Wall Street to Hollywood Boulevard have found themselves "unin-tentionally childless." One study showed that 49 percent of women ages twenty-eight to fifty-five who earned $100,000 or more annually were childless. However, only 14 percent of them wanted to live their lives that way. They put so much emphasis on their careers that they inadvertently ended up alone.[1]

Successful women tell us that there are a number of factors that play a part in this cultural trend. These women blamed their demanding work schedules, which included weekends, and made it difficult to sustain romantic relationships. Some said that men with big egos did not want to marry overachieving women, while others stated that promotions were hard to come by if the boss detected marriage- or baby-hunger. Many simply said that it just never seemed like the right time to develop a romance or start a family.

No matter the reason, the message these loveless, childless executives send to their younger sisters is "Don't get so caught up in your career track that you do not have a bigger plan and thus miss out on the other blessings of life."

A HEALTHY FOCUS ON CAREER IS GOOD

Please do not misunderstand what we are trying to say here. We are very much in favor of singles finding their vocational call and preparing for it. A balanced focus on one's career is a good thing. In fact, it can be healthy for a marriage if the couple knows who they are and what they want to do in life. It can be a positive thing to achieve a level of educational or career success before you marry. Taking this idea too far, however, can cause you to get your priorities out of line. You can focus so much on your career that you ignore other equally important issues, such as finding a lifetime partner and building a family. And women are not the only ones who are guilty of putting too much emphasis on career.

BRANDON'S STORY

Brandon was a thirty-nine-year-old director of a nonprofit mission in the inner city who put in long hours ministering to the poor and leading them to Christ. While he was placing too much emphasis on his career, he was not trying to accumulate wealth or status. He was dedicated to his work because he felt a strong call to serve the Lord.

Brandon grew up in a stable Christian home, and his parents were a great example of Christian service. They were at church every time the doors were opened and volunteered for every committee they could. His dad had been a deacon in the church as far back as Brandon could remember, and his mom taught Sunday school. He followed their example.

Brandon focused so much on his career that he even moved into the transitional house at the mission so that he could be closer to the people. While he enjoyed the freedom he had as a single man, as he got older, he noticed it was not as fulfilling as it once had been. He watched couples at church and started to envy the care they had for one another. His desire for a family grew, but Brandon did not date, go to singles groups, or socialize in circles where he could meet single women. The only time he was around available women was when he occasionally taught the singles Sunday school class at his church.

When I asked him why he did not socialize or date, he said that he had sworn off singles groups because they were a pool of desperate women and predatory men. He said single women today wanted to find a man who would take care of them financially and labeled dating as distracting, draining, and unrewarding. Besides, if he gave up such a diversion, he could spend more time serving the Lord. I suspected that Brandon's judgmental attitude about singles groups, and dating in general, was covering up a deeper hurt, which I needed to explore.

Brandon was truly doing what the Lord put him on earth to do. It was inspiring to hear him talk, with great passion, about how he helped people get on their feet and find the Lord. The problem was some of his motivation was unhealthy. Many of the singles we see in counseling learn that their motivation for career and success is not completely healthy.

A MATTER OF PRIORITIES AND PURPOSE

Rick Warren, in *The Purpose-Driven Life*, says, "Nothing matters more than knowing God's purposes for your life, nothing can compensate for that—not success, wealth, fame, or pleasure. Without a purpose, life is trivial, petty, and pointless."[2] If you place too much emphasis on career and success you may not have the total picture of your divine purpose. The singles in this chapter were focusing on only a part of their divine purpose: their careers. They left little or no room for the Lord to guide them in other areas.

Erica, Emily, and Brandon all realized that they focused on career for several unhealthy reasons. They told us:

1. Their careers were something they could control. They could not control whether someone loved them or not. They could control how much energy they spent on work.
2. They were more successful at their careers than they were at love. These singles said that they were good at work and bad at love. They simply put their energy into those areas where they did well, in order to feel good about themselves.
3. Their careers were something that they could count on to reward them. Love and marriage were not. They could count on the fact that working hard in their careers would result in a certain level of success. However, hard work in the area of love and marriage did not necessarily yield positive results. To quote Emily, "Why should I work that hard for nothing when I can put that much

energy into work and get great financial and emotional rewards?"

According to Rick Warren, the average person is driven by one or more of the following unhealthy motivators:[3]

- Guilt
- Resentment
- Materialism
- The need for approval

Erica, Emily, and Brandon could safely say that a degree of unhealthy motivation kept them from finding their total purpose in life, which just might have included a mate. Unfortunately, it is easy for singles today to get their priorities out of focus. Most of the singles advice books in both the secular and Christian markets tell you to focus on your vocational path, know where you are going, use your gifts, and be the best you can be.

Author Sam Keen, in *To Love and Be Loved*, says it is best to know where you are going, and then figure out who you want to join you. Josh Harris, in his book *I Kissed Dating Goodbye*, says that dating in many cases distracts adults from their primary responsibility of preparing for the future. These authors were trying to caution singles not to let relationships distract them from pursuing their dreams. This is sound advice, but many singles take it too far.

Erica, Emily, and Brandon didn't want their dating relationships to distract them from developing their careers. They inadvertently let their quest for vocational satisfaction distract them from the pursuit of marriage and family. It isn't wise to let love relationships derail you from your career, but it is equally unwise to let your career derail you from finding the mate the Lord has for you.

As Emily and Erica started to heal, it took a lot of effort for them to stop placing so much importance on their careers. They had to take time away from their busy lives to be available to men and get back into the dating scene. In some ways it is harder for women because in most singles groups the demographics show that there are at least two women for every man. But Erica and Emily stayed the course and began to date again. They met some interesting men, as well as others who were not so interesting, and managed to form friendships along the way. Erica met a man whom she is now dating steadily, a motivational speaker she heard speak at a seminar at work. You will never guess what his topic was: "How to Put More Play and Less Work in Your Life." This was a sure sign to Erica that she had found someone special. Emily is continuing to work on developing healthy dating and mating patterns and believes that God has a plan for her love life.

Brandon did not set out to make his career his top priority—he just wanted to be more established before marrying. Apparently Brandon's parents married young and struggled a lot vocationally and economically. Like many parents, they did not want him to have to struggle, so they constantly encouraged him to get established and repeatedly warned him of the stresses he would otherwise endure. While it was noble for his parents to want more for their children, there are great lessons we learn through struggle.

THE VALUE OF MARITAL STRUGGLES

A lot of singles today tell us that they want to start their marriages with more than their parents had. They want a car, a house, and the beginning of a substantial stock portfolio before they marry. They do not want to struggle through the rigors of school or suffer from poverty as they build assets. This mind-set is not new. As far back as the mid-1800s single men had to have a parcel of the family's land and be capable of farming it in order to seek a wife. Throughout history, the standard of entering marriage with some degree of success, wealth, or status is typical. We just believe that singles today are taking this philosophy to an extreme.

Brandon wanted to get all of the difficult things out of the way so that when he got married, life would be easier. But he, like many of today's singles, didn't realize that the Lord may want to teach him through the very struggles he was trying to avoid. Sometimes the struggle to build something together, such as a house, a career, or a ministry, is exactly what a couple needs to mature.

Singles today may actually be missing out on great growth opportunities because they believe they should get all of the difficult things out of the way before they say "I do." This can also be a mistake because we tend to become more set in our ways after building a career or establishing a measure of success. We are less moldable, which makes it difficult to learn the necessary lessons that marriage teaches. Tom and I are glad for the hardships that we had to endure in the early years of our marriage, because they molded and shaped us into better people.

OUR EARLY MARITAL STRUGGLES

When Tom and I first married, we were poor college students. I graduated from college with $250 to my name. Tom was flat broke, because he had spent all of his money enrolling in graduate school. We used to quote the old Southern saying, "We are as poor as Job's turkey." Who knows, perhaps the turkey had more than we did! It was exactly this struggle of clipping coupons, managing a tight budget, and shopping at thrift stores that grew us as people, developed our faith, and strengthened our union.

Like most couples, we married our opposite. We were

especially polarized in the financial department. Tom was a spender, and I was a saver. He would say to me, "You pinch a penny until Lincoln's eyes pop out." Because of our differences, we had many conflicts over money. We did not fight fairly, so we had to learn—the hard way.

The difficulties of us both establishing our careers also strengthened us as individuals and as a couple. We had to learn to give and take. Sometimes Tom's career took precedence, and sometimes mine did. We learned to put each other's needs above our own, when to sacrifice, and when to ask for our needs to be met. Not only did this help us as a married couple but it matured us as people. Learning to resolve conflict and reconcile our differences were some of the most valuable lessons of our lives. Much of the material we teach others today was born out of our early marital struggles. If we had not experienced this time, the Soul Healing Love Model may never have been developed.

BRANDON'S HEALING

Brandon began to understand that there are valuable lessons learned in relationship struggles. He began to see God's plan and submit to His leading, rather than trying to control the areas where he felt adequate and successful. He began to ask the Lord what He wanted for him in the areas of dating and mating. The Scripture passage in Ephesians 3:20 became a theme: "God can do anything, you know—far more than you could ever imagine or guess or request in your wildest dreams!"(MSG) He began to see that the Lord had a divine purpose for his love life as well as his call to Christian service.

Brandon went even further to say that too much emphasis on one's call to serve the Lord just might get in the way of serving Him. He realized that his focus on serving the Lord with his career had become too consuming. In counseling, Brandon said that deep in his heart he felt hopeless that he would ever find a mate who could support his career choice. His hopelessness was the result of a very painful breakup that had happened several years earlier.

Brandon had been engaged to a beautiful woman who eventually broke up with him because she could not deal with his life's work at the mission. She thought that it was too dangerous, demanding, and consuming. Within a year of the breakup, she rebounded and married a well-off attorney. This crushed Brandon, and he developed a skepticism about women and marriage. It was no wonder that he was so judgmental and down on singles groups and the dating scene. His judgmental facade was hiding deep pain.

I suggested to Brandon that, while his busyness and extreme dedication to his career were noble, some of this might be an effort to hide his true feelings. "What feelings?" he asked. I replied, "Your painful feelings about being rejected and hurt by your fiancée when she broke up with you and married someone else. I think you even fear it happening again, so you protect yourself with busyness." Brandon tried to deny this and say it was in the past, but his tears betrayed him.

"You're right," he admitted at last. "I have been hurt and afraid since that painful breakup. It was so difficult for me that I buried myself in work and closed a part of my heart to women. And I have to confess that I have been resentful toward the Lord for what happened."

Brandon's frustration caused him to wonder if God was calling him to be single, but the thought of being alone and celibate was very distasteful to him. Brandon also thought that if he was called to be single, then God would take the desire to be married away. However, this was not happening. There are some people who are indeed called to be single, but that doesn't mean you should assume this applies to you because your heart is broken or because you are skeptical of the opposite sex. After counseling and much prayer, Brandon realized that he was not called to be single. He simply had a lack of faith that the Lord would provide a soul mate for him.

Brandon's lack of faith made him fear rejection. This caused him to appear distant, superior, and judgmental to women, especially if he felt the slightest attraction. When he would meet someone he was attracted to, he would immediately feel insecure and brag about the work he did at the mission.

When he taught the singles' Sunday school, he typically used himself as an example, fancying himself much like the apostle Paul, his role model for Christian service. He did not realize that this was a turnoff to women. He earned a reputation for having high standards and being hard to please. His married friends said that they did not know anyone to set him up with who would be good enough for him. This bothered him, but he did not know how to change until he came into counseling.

With our help, he learned that he had adapted to his broken heart by developing pride in his career. This realization helped Brandon heal from the wounds of the broken relationship with his fiancée and trust the Lord to find a soul mate for him. Consequently, several things changed in his life. He stopped using his career to compensate for his loneliness, and he started doing more social activities at church. Most importantly, he started to balance his focus on career with his search for a soul mate.

When we last saw Brandon he was actively involved with his church singles group and dating a wonderful woman named Stephanie, who respected his career and encouraged him to pursue his call. Stephanie came to the mission and worked alongside Brandon, ministered to the children in the neighborhood, and taught a women's Bible study. Brandon and Stephanie were taking their relationship slowly and asking the Lord to guide them every step of the way.

MAKING IT PRACTICAL: WHAT ABOUT YOU?

After reading this chapter, do you think that the Lord might be telling you that you are placing too much emphasis on your career? Do you busy yourself with work-related activities or Christian service so that you will not have to deal with loneliness? Ask the Lord for guidance in showing you His plan for your life and your soul mate. Trust Him to do it, and He will.

FOR FURTHER THOUGHT

1. How much emphasis do you place on career, success, and call?

2. Has your motivation in your career ever been unhealthy?

3. Are there things you can do to develop a healthy balance between work and play?

GROWING YOUR FAITH

- God is in control of every area of my life and I can surrender even the areas where I don't feel confident.

  > What is faith? It is the confident assurance that something we want is going to happen. It is the certainty that what we hope for is waiting for us, even though we cannot see it up ahead. (Hebrews 11:1, TLB)

- God may have something important to teach me through struggle.

> We can rejoice, too, when we run into problems and trials, for we know that they are good for us — they help us learn to be patient. And patience develops strength of character in us and helps us trust God more each time we use it until finally our hope and faith are strong and steady. (Romans 5:3-4, TLB)

- God's divine purpose for my life encompasses every area, including my career and my love life.

> The steps of a good man are ordered by the LORD,
> And He delights in his way. (Psalm 37:23)

Concern That the Marriage Will Fail

I don't want to get divorced

Jack and Christy came to counseling because they had been dating for two years and really wanted to get married, but couldn't seem to take the final step. They were both in their midtwenties and their parents told them that perhaps they should wait until they were older and could be more sure. The problem was they *had* been waiting—for so long that they felt stuck.

"How can we be sure we are not making a mistake?" Christy questioned.

"How do you know that your marriage will last?" Jack asked.

"How can you be certain that you have picked the right mate?" Christy echoed.

These were only a few of the many questions that prompted this couple to come to counseling.

More and more singles like Jack and Christy are coming into counseling before they get engaged in an effort to determine if their relationship is right for them. Relationship counseling is different from premarital counseling because the couple actually comes to determine if they are healthy and compatible enough to move forward to engagement and eventually marriage. Tom and I think relationship counseling is a smart move for a couple. We complimented Jack and Christy on their wise choice and worked with them to help them feel more secure about their mate selection as well as their relationship.

Both Jack and Christy came from divorced homes, which made them fear they would suffer the same fate. To complicate matters, both sets of parents were quite negative about marriage and not very supportive of Jack and Christy. Despite their parents' views, Jack and Christy were still holding on to a positive notion of marriage, if only by a thread.

We are seeing a trend toward a more optimistic view of marriage among younger singles. In Generation Y (those born between 1979 and 1994), the number of marriages is rising, a trend that author Pamela Paul calls *matrimania*. Paul feels that these young singles are marrying in response to their observations of those in Generation X (those born between 1965 and 1978), many of whom are getting older and not marrying.[1] It appears that Gen Yers like Jack and Christy do not want to grow old alone like their older brothers and sisters seem poised to do.

Paul quotes research from a 1997 poll that shows nine out of ten twenty-somethings said that a happy marriage is part of their ideal life. In the minds of most twenty-somethings, marriage ranks higher than career. They consider being a good wife or mother a sign of success, place paramount importance on family togetherness, and believe that it is critical for children today to have activities that anchor them to their families, like regular sit-down dinners or weekly religious services.[2]

We are glad that the younger generation is getting a better image of marriage, family, and faith. We are pleased that the idea of marriage and childbearing within marriage is coming back in vogue with this younger crowd, but there is a concern here. Paul found that many of these early marriages are ending in divorce, most of them before the birth of children and often within the first five years. She calls these *starter marriages*.[3]

As a dedicated married couple, there is something about this term that grates on our nerves. We believe in starter homes, starter loans, and even starter bicycles, but starter marriages sounds almost profane! Marriage is for keeps, and Gen Yers need to have this notion firmly planted in their brains. Unfortunately, Jack and Christy were so afraid that their marriage would fail that they had trouble embracing this.

Jack was scared because, not only did his parents have a painful divorce but all of his aunts and uncles were divorced as well. Jack was fearful, so he kept coming up with reasons why he could not propose. He said he needed to get a house, build up his sales territory, and secure a promotion before he could feel comfortable asking Christy to be his wife.

Jack's fear of getting married caused Christy to question whether Jack was the right one for her. They were so terri-fied that their relationship would fail that they were thinking about moving in together to try things out before taking the final step. Apparently, several family members, including Jack's parents (who were not Christians), were pushing them to do this to "see if they were compatible." Their friends and family suggested cohabitation, to not only save money for the wedding but also "test-drive" their marriage. This concept of experiment-ing with trial marriage has been pervasive in our culture for the last two decades. Unfortunately, it has not proven to help with marital success.

In *Why Is Marriage Important?* Michael Craven says,

Many people falsely believe that living together prior to marriage serves as an effective 'testing ground' for marriage, thereby increasing the couple's chance for a long term, healthy marriage. However, four decades of sociological evidence overwhelmingly demonstrated that just the opposite is true.[4]

Dr. Linda Waite and Dr. Maggie Gallagher, in their book *A Case for Marriage*, caused quite a stir with the results of their research, which suggest that cohabiting couples are less financially stable, less faithful, and less happy than their lawfully wedded counterparts. Live-in couples also have rockier marriages and a significantly higher divorce rate, up to 48 percent higher than couples who do not cohabit.[5] Pamela Paul says that trial marriages cause couples to place "the Me above the Us, the If above the When, the Now above Forever."[6] She further states that these couples typically do not share bank accounts, insurance policies, tax forms, or investment portfolios. They often maintain separate social lives as well.

As we shared these findings with Jack and Christy, they confessed that they really did not think that cohabiting was such a wise or godly idea, but they felt pressure from their parents and friends and thought it might push them further toward marriage. The Scripture is clear that cohabitation is not the answer: "Marriage is honorable among all, and the bed undefiled; but fornicators and adulterers God will judge" (Hebrews 13:4). With some prayerful counsel, Jack and Christy were able to see that even if there were economic or relational reasons to cohabit, this was not what God desired for them.

With this issue finally settled, they were able to move forward and look at skills for building their marriage. In counseling, we teach five keys to building a successful marriage. We have seen that if couples use these keys, they feel more secure about moving ahead to engagement and marriage.

KEYS TO MARITAL SUCCESS

1. Practice healthy mate selection and seek God for His choice for you.
2. Learn all that you can about developing the skills of a healthy marriage.
3. Keep the Lord the center of your union.
4. Sign up for keeps. Do not consider divorce as an option.
5. Commit to being a soul healer in your marriage.

KEY #1: PRACTICE HEALTHY MATE SELECTION

Often we are asked, "How will I know if I have found the right mate?" When I was young, I was told that when I met "the one," I would just know that he was right. This was the romantic notion that I heard from many of my family members. The problem was that they were divorced, so their credibility was tainted. In my heart, I really wanted to believe them. I tried hard to subscribe to this ethereal ideal. I even put up posters in my dorm room with romantic sayings like "Think not that you can direct the course of love, for love, if if finds you worthy, it will direct your course."[7] I pondered such poetic prose as "From every human being there rises a light that reaches straight to heaven. When two souls that are destined to be together find each other, their streams of light flow together." [8] I was forever looking for that "stream of light," but it seemed I always ended up in a dark alley.

My pastor tried to help by giving me a more spiritual take on mate selection. He said to pray about it and ask God specifically for His will for my mate and the path would become clear. As a new Christian, I was not sure how to hear God's voice and was much too fearful of making a mistake. A cacophony of white noise rang in my ears as I tried to pray about whether I should marry Tom.

All of these people were well meaning, but I was simply too wounded by the many divorces in my family to feel certain about my choice for a mate. Unfortunately, we see many singles every year, including Jack and Christy, who share the same feelings. They too were told by many that when they found their true love, they would feel certain. The problem with this naive, romantic sentiment is that it sets singles up to be disappointed. Many of them strive for this great feeling of confidence and are frustrated, even devastated, when it does not happen. They doubt themselves, romance, and even the Lord.

It is easy for singles to get confused when trying to seek the voice and heart of God. We now know how easy it is to mistake brain chemicals for true love. The overwhelming feelings that brain chemicals provide can make people think they have found the one God has for them. Perfectionist daters can easily miss "Mr. or Ms. Right" because they are holding out for something better and are sure that God would not want them to "settle." Because of this, singles should learn all that they can about healthy mate selection in order to make sure that they are not falling prey to common mistakes. We encouraged Jack and Christy to find helpful couples' resources on mate selection.

BOOKS, TAPES, DISKS, AND PROGRAMS

As we speak across the country and the globe, we continue to find excellent books, tapes, CDs, and DVDs on how to find the partner who is right for you. Many of the materials we have found are referenced in this book. Programs designed to help singles make the right choice for a mate are popping up everywhere. One of the most popular aides to finding a mate is an online dating service. The good news is that many online dating services require you to complete a detailed personality profile, which helps you learn more about yourself. You also have to complete an explicit list of what you desire in a mate in order to find someone with whom you are most compatible.

One of the best-known services is eHarmony, started by author and psychologist Dr. Neil Clark Warren. This service has helped many people not only get to know themselves but also to find a soul mate. Tom and I credit the lengthy self-analysis as a key part of this service's success.

Many of these programs, including eHarmony, select matches based on issues such as similar faith, values, goals, family backgrounds, age, and educational experiences. Studies show that singles who are compatible on these issues have a better chance of making their relationships last. Regardless of how you feel about Internet dating, completing these profiles can help you make a better, more informed decision regarding a spouse. Obviously, Jack and Christy did not need an online dating service, but they could greatly benefit from taking some of the personality and relationship inventories. We offered them a chance to do this in relationship counseling.

RELATIONSHIP AND PERSONALITY INVENTORIES

Often premarital counseling done by pastors or counselors includes at least three sessions in which the couple is given a relationship or personality inventory. There are many good ones out there today. The PREPARE inventory by Dr. David Olson, SYMBIS (Saving Your Marriage Before It Starts) by Drs. Les and Leslie Parrott, FOCCUS, a Catholic relationship inventory, and the Taylor-Johnson Temperament Analysis are designed specifically for engaged couples to see what their differences are and where their strengths lie. These are only a few of the premarital programs that help couples determine the areas in their relationship that need work. I used several of these tools with Jack and Christy, which enabled them to see their relationship more objectively and determine their compatibility.

Inventories can also pave the way for premarital counseling, which studies show can improve marital satisfaction and prevent divorce. Good premarital counseling covers the issues that couples typically fight about and that can lead to divorce: money, sex, roles, child rearing, in-laws, religion, and jealousy over time spent outside the marriage. Premarital counseling helps couples learn to recognize potential conflicts in these difficult areas and to find common ground about them before they walk down the aisle. It is also a good place to learn the skills of marriage. Once the couple learns more about themselves and their relationship, they are better prepared for a lifetime commitment.

KEY #2: DEVELOP THE SKILLS OF A HEALTHY MARRIAGE

Like many singles, Jack and Christy had the popular impression that making marriage last was a mystical, magical process for the "lucky ones" who find true love. Our society has sold us on the idea that if you are in love, marriage should be effortless and romance will make everything easy. Buying into this false notion is a serious mistake.

As a married couple of almost thirty years and therapists for the last two and a half decades, we have discovered this profound bit of wisdom: *Marriage is not luck; it is skill!* Love is not a mystical emotion that we feel; it is a skill that is learned. Like any skill, it takes time and effort. Any ability that is worth developing requires energy, investment, and training. Unfortunately, it takes more training to get a driver's license in this country than it does to get a marriage license. Couples spend more time planning a wedding than they do planning their marriage.

We encourage singles like Jack and Christy to take the time

to get the training and learn the skills necessary to stay married. Both of them were in sales and regularly attended seminars on the skills of selling, so the idea of "learning the skills of marriage" was appealing to their intellect and soothed their fear. Fortunately, there are now many marriage education and training programs to choose from.

THE MARRIAGE EDUCATION BOOM

More and more pastors, rabbis, and priests are investing in marriage ministries in their churches. Marriage enrichment and education programs are starting in churches, synagogues, and schools. These programs provide numerous resources to parishioners and include marriage courses, retreats, and support groups. Marriage mentoring is also becoming popular. In these programs, young couples are assigned an older, wiser couple who befriend and walk along side of them. The mentoring couple's role is to support the newlyweds and show them the ropes of marriage.

For those couples who are not yet affiliated with a church or particular denomination, there are several online marriage education and resource groups. Here are several that we recommend:

www.SmartMarriages.com
www.RealRelationships.com (which includes the Saving
    Your Marriage Before It Starts program, or SYMBIS)
www.PrepareEnrich.com
www.covenantmarriage.com
www.AMFMonline.com (Association for Marriage and
    Family Ministries)
www.SoulHealingLove.com
www.ACODP.com (Adult Children of Divorced Parents)

Studies show that attending at least one marriage enrichment activity per year can help effect marital success. Tom and

I have helped start many marriage ministries and mentoring programs at churches in our hometown and across the country. Fortunately for Jack and Christy, they attended one of these churches, which had a thriving marriage ministry. They were fearful of attending because they were not yet married, but with a little push from us, they made the first step. Being around engaged and newly married couples was a great experience for them. They found it very encouraging to see happy couples who felt good about their decision to get married.

Tom and I do retreats where we take couples away and teach them communication tools and techniques from the Soul Healing Love Model. Jack and Christy came to one of our weekend retreats and it gave them even more confidence that they could succeed at marriage. Along with teaching marriage skills, we also share some of the groundbreaking research that has been published about marriage.

CURRENT MARRIAGE RESEARCH

Social scientists and therapists study marriage in order to remedy the high divorce rate in our country. We now have empirical research about what behaviors make marriages work and what makes them fail. The findings of these researchers have basically cracked the code to successful marital relationships. If couples heed these findings, they stand a better chance of making their marriage last. One of the premier researchers on marriage is Dr. John Gottman.

Dr. John Gottman, in his book *The Marriage Clinic*, shares the research he has done with married couples in his "love lab" at the University of Washington for the last twenty-five years. In his lab, couples come and live and are observed via hidden camera. These couples are also wired to biofeedback machines to determine their levels of stress as they interact. By studying the interactions of these couples, Dr. Gottman and his staff found that couples who exhibited certain unhealthy behaviors and styles of communication were more likely to divorce, and couples who had certain healthy communication styles were more apt to stay married.

Because of his extensive research, Dr. Gottman can predict with over 90 percent accuracy which of the couples who come into his lab will divorce and which ones will stay together. If couples will heed his advice, it has been empirically proven that they have a much greater likelihood of staying together for the long haul.

As we studied the good doctor's research, we made an amazing discovery. What he and his team of behavior scientists found was actually written in the book of Proverbs! This ancient book of Hebrew wisdom mirrors Dr. Gottman's research in a remarkable way. So by following the knowledge and advice contained in Proverbs, couples can predict their marital success to a statistically significant degree.

This was so amazing to us that we began teaching Proverbs, in conjunction with empirical marital research, to our workshop participants. Typically we teach from *The Living Bible* because it is written in a language that couples can understand. We taught this material to Jack and Christy, and they were awed at how research proved what the Scriptures instructed so long ago. They were also glad that they were learning skills that were not only scriptural but also proven to make marriages successful. Jack and Christy both stated that learning these tried-and-true skills was one of the most helpful things they did to feel confident that their marriage would not fail. They thought that every couple should know them. In their honor, we are giving you just a small preview of what this precious couple learned.

Gottman's Predictors of Divorce[9]

Criticism. Couples who are critical of one another are more likely to divorce than are non-critical couples. Dr. Gottman found that although it is healthy to bring up difficult issues in the marriage, couples need to do so in a soft, loving manner, not in a harsh, critical way. Proverbs 15:4 says, "Gentle words cause life and health; griping brings discouragement" (TLB).

Stonewalling. Couples who stonewall each other, refuse to discuss issues, or withdraw from conflict by sweeping things under the rug increase their chances of divorce. This is because their difficult issues do not get resolved, and resentment grows in the marriage. Proverbs clearly teaches us that not addressing problems can cause trouble in relationships: "It is an honor to receive a frank reply" (Proverbs 24:26, TLB).

Defensiveness. Couples who are defensive and blind to the part they play in a conflict divorce at a much higher rate than those who are not. Proverbs 13:3 states, "Self-control means controlling the tongue! A quick retort can ruin everything" (TLB).

Contempt. This emotion is defined as a disdain or lack of respect for one's partner. When you feel contempt, you actually start to despise him or her and wonder if there is something wrong with your partner's character rather than simply his or her behavior. According to Proverbs 10:12, "Hatred stirs old quarrels, but love overlooks insults" (TLB).

Gottman's Predictors of Marital Success[10]

Repair Attempts. Gottman's research shows that all couples fight, and the presence of conflict is not a predictor of divorce. However, couples who make frequent attempts to repair the relationship after a conflict have a better chance of staying married. In Proverbs 13:2, Solomon reminds us that "the good man wins his case by careful argument; the evil-minded only wants to fight" (TLB).

Accepting Influence. This means considering what your part- ner might think and weighing his or her opinion as equal to your own. It also involves receiving criticism. The writers of Proverbs have much to say about foolish people who do not receive criticism or accept influence. Proverbs 13:18 declares, "If you refuse criticism you will end in poverty and disgrace" (TLB).

Soft Versus Hard Start-Up. Couples who start their conflicts in a calm, rational, and soft manner make marriages that last. For example, instead of saying, "I can't believe you're so careless that you don't record your checks in the register," say, "Things would run more smoothly if you would record your checks." In Proverbs 15:1, Solomon states, "A gentle answer turns away wrath, but harsh words cause quarrels" (TLB).

More Positive Than Negative Comments. When spouses speak more about their partner's positive attributes than about their negative, they increase their marriage's success rate. According to Proverbs 19:22, "Kindness makes a man [or woman] attractive" (TLB).

Jack and Christy found that learning these proven marriage skills and practicing them actually improved their relationship. They also saw that all of these great skills could be learned by reading the Proverbs. There are thirty-one chapters in the book of Proverbs, approximately one for each day of the month. We encourage couples like Jack and Christy to make a habit of sharing a chapter with each other each day. After doing this for several months, Jack said, "Just think of all the time and energy Dr. Gottman and his eager team of researchers would have saved if they had regularly read the wisdom written in the book of Proverbs." He was right. Jack realized that marriage is indeed a skill that can be learned, especially by reading the Scriptures.

KEY #3: KEEP THE LORD THE CENTER OF YOUR UNION

Jack and Christy were aware that developing a Christ-centered marriage was one of the greatest things they could do in their lives. Christ is the glue that keeps a couple together, especially through the hard times. They also knew that, unfortunately, being a Christian has not proven to prevent divorce. The divorce rate in the church hit 57 percent before it declined. This was actually greater than the secular divorce rate at that time, a statistic that further fueled Jack and Christy's fear. It is a sad commentary that being a Christian doesn't immunize couples against divorce. However, practicing their faith daily, in concert with the other steps we encouraged them to take, would go a long way to help them.

KEY #4: SIGN UP FOR KEEPS

You have read throughout this book how marriage is no longer viewed by our culture as a permanent endeavor. This attitude has made it easy for couples to throw in the towel. To combat this, there is a movement afoot to establish covenant marriages as a legal category. The March 2004 issue of *Psychology Today* featured an article titled "Covenant Marriage: A New Marital Contract," which states that a covenant marriage is not easily broken, and the only grounds for immediate divorce are adultery or abuse. In a covenant marriage, a couple would have to wait two years before divorcing and commit to seek counseling from a therapist who believes in marriage. Covenant marriages reflect the biblical concept of matrimony, so it is no surprise that the author of this article found that most covenant couples considered themselves conservative or religious.[11]

There is now an official covenant marriage movement, which was established in 1999. It consists of churches, marriage ministries, political groups, and lawmakers who desire to restore the sacredness of marriage and have couples make the choice to marry "till death do us part." Because of this effort, the state of Louisiana adopted a covenant marriage law in which couples have the option for a covenant marriage or a standard marriage contract. To the surprise of liberal lawmakers, many young couples are choosing the covenant option. Other states are now looking into this and longitudinal studies are underway to see if covenant marriages last.

We shared the covenant marriage option with Jack and Christy. While they did not have this as a legal option in our state of North Carolina, it was a spiritual option. They were very much in favor of this because it was biblically sound. While it put pressure on them to be sure of their relationship, they did not want to commit to marriage if it was not going to be forever. They realized that making a covenant would give them the stamina to stick with marriage through the inevitable struggles that occur.

KEY #5: COMMIT TO BEING A SOUL HEALER IN YOUR MARRIAGE

One of the most important things we shared with Jack and Christy is that they were wounded and in need of healing. We learned earlier in this book that all of us have soul wounds that are inflicted upon us by society, peers, and our family of origin. These soul wounds *will* be triggered in our marriage. We have one or two choices. We can lament about how difficult it is to deal with a wounded spouse who wounds us, or we can see that God gave us marriage so that we can transcend our selfish natures and be a healing to each other.

This soul healing is not the codependent "healing" done by unhealthy couples who want to "fix" each other in order to control each other. It is seeing the woundedness within ourselves and realizing that the Lord is healing us with His unconditional love. We allow God's love to spill onto our partner and heal him or her as well. This makes the unavoidable struggles in marriage something to embrace rather than avoid.

We developed the Soul Healing Love Model because we believe that marriage is a replica of our relationship with God and a place where healing the soul can occur. If couples choose to be soul healers, then marriage becomes an arena for them to work out issues within their hearts and lives and to give and receive healing. The motivation for giving your partner soul-healing love is the fact that we have so graciously been given the same love from God. The result is that soul-healing love imitates the oneness we feel with God; our love for our spouse and his or her love for us will help restore us to wholeness.

The concept of soul-healing love is found in Scripture in Ephesians 5:25: "Husbands, love your wives, just as Christ also loved the church and gave Himself for her." Verse 33 of the same chapter says, "Nevertheless let each one of you in particular so love his own wife as himself, and let the wife see that she respects her husband." Galatians 6:2 says, "Bear one another's burdens, and so fulfill the law of Christ." Many of the aspects of soul-healing love replicate the ideal of love in 1 Corinthians:

Love suffers long and is kind; love does not envy; love does not parade itself, is not puffed up; does not behave rudely, does not seek its own, is not provoked, thinks no evil; does not rejoice in iniquity, but rejoices in the truth; bears all things, believes all things, hopes all things, endures all things. (13:4-7)

With this kind of love in mind, marriage then becomes a form of therapy where each spouse plays the role of patient and healer. Harville Hendrix, in *Keeping the Love You Find*, says, "Marriage itself is in essence therapy, and your partner's needs chart your path to psychological and spiritual wholeness."[12] This therapy or healing model of marriage is supported by many relationship theorists. Jay Adams says that one of the main goals of marriage is mutual sanctification, with each partner sharpening the other and making him or her more Christlike through the trials and struggles that couples endure. Tom and I speak of marriage as a "moral crucible" for couples. A crucible is a severe test or trial designed to cause lasting change. It is the struggles of marriage that form this crucible.

Husbands and wives who have the Lord to guide them and His love to inspire them can face this crucible. We are capable of soul-healing love only through the power of Jesus Christ. We have developed several tools that are designed to make soul-healing love more practical and doable. These techniques are simple but not easy. They are simple to do, but the motivation has to come from a place of "want to."

"Want to" is the strong desire to be a healing agent to your spouse, because you see it as part of your divine purpose. When times are hard, you want to. When you are not getting your own needs met, you want to. When things are unfair, still you want to. In a soul-healing marriage, you desire to heal because you want to.

JACK AND CHRISTY'S STORY

Jack and Christy wanted to see the positives of marriage instead of all of the negatives. They saw that marriage is a gift from God designed to help individuals grow into the people He has called them to be. They realized that while it takes work and commitment, it can be done. As they worked with us, they overcame the hesitations and fears they had about getting and staying married. We watched as Jack and Christy defied their fears and made a choice to commit to marriage. They felt confident that their marriage would last because they would choose to make it last.

It was such a delight to hear them exchange their wedding vows. They deliberately chose a covenant marriage with the traditional wedding vows from the *Common Book of Prayer*. They vowed to stay together "for better for worse, for richer for poorer, in sickness and in health, till death do us part." Their friends, family, and proud therapists stood in awe as this brave couple looked at each other, with trembling lips and glistening eyes, and poured out their hearts of commitment to one another and God. When they said, "We will be together 'till death do us part,'" they meant it.

I can't explain the awe, pride, and exuberance I felt in being their counselor, coach, and mentor, as I watched them make one of the most frightening, yet profound, decisions of their lives. They possessed the confidence they needed and the spiritual, emotional, and relational tools to make their marriage last. Jack and Christy trusted God to help them overcome their fear that their marriage would fail, and He did.

MAKING IT PRACTICAL: WHAT ABOUT YOU?

Do you fear that your marriage will end in divorce? Ask God to help you reprogram your fear and trust Him that you will someday have a healthy, godly marriage. Trust Him to do it, and He will.

FOR FURTHER THOUGHT

1. Have you experienced fear that your future marriage will end in divorce?

2. We believe that marriage is skill, not luck. How do you respond to the idea of learning the keys to marital success?

3. To what in your life have you devoted significant energy, investment, and training? Do you think it was time well spent?

GROWING YOUR FAITH

- I can choose to have a covenant marriage.

   "In the original creation, God made male and female to be together. Because of this, a man leaves father and mother, and in marriage he becomes one flesh with a woman — no longer two individuals, but forming a new unity." (Mark 10:6-8, MSG)

- I can have a successful marriage if I keep Christ at the center.

    What is clearest to me is the way Christ treats the church. And this provides a good picture of how each husband is to treat his wife, loving himself in loving her, and how each wife is to honor her husband. (Ephesians 5:32-33, MSG)

- God's love will enable me to be a soul healer to my future spouse.

    Husbands, go all out in your love for your wives, exactly as Christ did for the church — a love marked by giving, not getting. Christ's love makes the church whole. His words evoke her beauty. (Ephesians 5:25-26, MSG)

Notes

INTRODUCTION

1. S. Michael Craven, *Why Is Marriage Important? The Reasonable Defense of Marriage* (Cincinnati: National Coalition for the Protection of Children and Families, 2003), 2.

REASON #1: SKEPTICISM ABOUT LOVE AND MARRIAGE

1. United States Bureau of the Census, "Households, Families, Marital Status and Living Arrangements" (Washington, DC: Department of Vital Statistics, United States Government Printing Office, 2004), 1.
2. Jen Abbas, *Generation Ex: Adult Children of Divorce and the Healing of Our Pain* (Colorado Springs, CO: Waterbrook, 2004), 1.
3. David Popenoe and Barbara Whitehead, "Why Men Can't Commit," *The State of Our Unions Report* (New Brunswick, NJ: Rutgers, 2002), 7–15.
4. Centers for Disease Control, "Cohabitation, Marriage, Divorce and Remarriage in the United States" 23 (22) (Hyattsville, MD: Department of Health and Human Services, 2002), 2.

5. David Popenoe and Barbara Whitehead, "The Marrying Kind: Which Men Marry and Why," *The State of Our Unions Report* (New Brunswick, NJ: Rutgers, 2004), 7–10.

6. Christina Nehring, "Mr. Goodbar Redux: Illusions. Affectations. Lies. This Is the Insidious and Incapacitating Legacy of Modern Dating Books," *Atlantic Monthly*, January 2002, 141.

7. Rose Sweet, *Dear God, Send Me a Soul Mate: Eight Steps for Finding a Spouse . . . God's Way* (Chattanooga, TN: AMG, 2002), 43.

REASON #2: LACK OF FAITH IN GOD'S PROVISION

1. Susan Jeffers, *Opening Our Hearts to Men: Learn to Let Go of Anger, Pain, and Loneliness and Create a Love That Works* (New York: Ballantine Books, 1990), 3.

2. David Popenoe and Barbara Whitehead, "Why Men Can't Commit," *The State of Our Unions Report* (New Brunswick, NJ: Rutgers, 2002), 3–7.

3. Thomas Moore, *Soul Mates: Honoring the Mysteries of Love and Relationship* (New York: Harper Perennial, 1994), xvii.

REASON #3: UNRESOLVED ISSUES FROM THE PAST

1. Steven Stosny, *The Powerful Self: A Workbook of Therapeutic Self-Empowerment* (New York: BookSurge, 2004), 71.

2. Harville Hendrix, *Keeping the Love You Find: A Guide for Singles* (New York: Pocket Books, 1992), 161.

3. Hendrix, 81–83.

4. Hendrix, 84–86.

5. Hendrix, 97–99.

6. Hendrix, 103–104.

7. Hendrix, 110–111.

8. Harville Hendrix, *Getting the Love You Want: A Guide for Couples* (New York: Harper Perennial, 1988), 50.

REASON #4: CONFUSION ABOUT THE RULES

1. Ellen K. Rothman, *Hands and Hearts: A History of Courtship in America* (Cambridge, MA: Harvard, 1984), 11.
2. www.suddenlysenior.com/courtingrituals.html.
3. Beth Bailey, *From Front Porch to Back Seat: Courtship in Twentieth-Century America* (Baltimore: John Hopkins, 1989), 13.
4. Pamela Paul, *The Starter Marriage and the Future of Matrimony* (New York: Villard, 2002), x–xvii.
5. Bailey, 2.
6. Augustus Napier, "Heroism, Men, and Marriage," *Journal of Marriage and Family Therapy* 17 (1991): 9.

REASON #5: POOR UNDERSTANDING OF THE PURPOSE OF MARRIAGE

1. Ellen K. Rothman, *Hands and Hearts: A History of Courtship in America* (Cambridge, MA: Harvard, 1984), 62.
2. S. Michael Craven, *Why Is Marriage Important? The Reasonable Defense of Marriage* (Cincinnati: National Coalition for the Protection of Children and Families, 2003), 2.
3. David Popenoe and Barbara Whitehead, "Why Men Can't Commit," *The State of Our Unions Report* (New Brunswick, NJ: Rutgers, 2002), 3.
4. Thomas Moore, *Soul Mates: Honoring the Mysteries of Love and Relationship* (New York: Harper Perennial, 1994), 93–94, 68.

5. John Gray, *Mars and Venus on a Date* (New York: HarperCollins, 1997), 128–129.

6. Popenoe and Whitehead, 3.

7. Linda Waite and Maggie Gallagher, in David Popenoe and Barbara Whitehead, "Why Men Can't Commit," *The State of Our Unions Report* (New Brunswick, NJ: Rutgers, 2002), 4–10.

8. Waite and Gallagher, 4–10.

REASON #6: FEAR OF GETTING HURT

1. Rick Warren, *The Purpose-Driven Life: What on Earth Am I Here For?* (Grand Rapids, MI: Zondervan, 2002), 110.

REASON #7: WANTING THE PERFECT MATE

1. Neil Clark Warren, PhD, *Finding the Love of Your Life: Ten Principles for Finding the Right Marriage Partner* (Colorado Springs, CO: Focus on the Family, 1998), 40.

2. Theresa L. Crenshaw, *The Alchemy of Love and Lust: How Hormones Influence Our Relationships* (New York: Simon & Schuster, 1996), 53.

3. Patricia Love, *The Truth About Love: The Highs, the Lows, and How You Can Make It Last Forever* (New York: Simon & Schuster, 2001), 32–33.

4. David Givens and Timothy Perper, in Helen Fisher, *Anatomy of Love: The Mysteries of Mating and Marriage and Why We Stray* (New York: Ballantine Books, 1992), 24–27.

5. Crenshaw, xxv.

6. Crenshaw, 4.

REASON #8: NOT DEALING WITH PRIOR HEARTBREAK

1. Mark McMinn, *Psychology, Theology, and Spirituality in Christian Counseling* (Forest, VA: American Association of

Christian Counselors Publications, 1996), 41.

2. Beverly and Tom Rodgers, *Adult Children of Divorced Parents: Making Your Marriage Work* (San Jose, CA: Resource Publications, 2002), 82.

3. "for," *Webster's College Dictionary* (New York: Random House, 1995), 519.

4. "give," *Webster's College Dictionary* (New York: Random House, 1995), 565.

REASON #9: AN UNBALANCED FOCUS ON CAREER

1. Sylvia Ann Hewlett, *Creating a Life: Professional Women and the Quest for Children* (New York: Talk Marimax Books, 2002), 28.

2. Rick Warren, *The Purpose-Driven Life: What on Earth Am I Here For?* (Grand Rapids, MI: Zondervan, 2002), 30.

3. Warren, 27–29.

REASON #10: CONCERN THAT THE MARRIAGE WILL FAIL

1. Pamela Paul, *The Starter Marriage and the Future of Matrimony* (New York: Villard, 2002), x–xvii.

2. Paul, xii–xiii.

3. Paul, xiii.

4. S. Michael Craven, *Why Is Marriage Important? The Reasonable Defense of Marriage* (Cincinnati: National Coalition for the Protection of Children and Families, 2003), 2.

5. Linda Waite and Maggie Gallagher, *A Case for Marriage: Why Married People Are Happier, Healthier, and Better Off Financially* (New York: Doubleday, 2000), 55.

6. Paul, 12.

7. Kahlil Gibran, *The Prophet* (New York: Knopf, 1952), 10.

8. Baal Shem Tov, quoted in *Apple Seeds*, Volume 18, #8 (April 2003), http://www.appleseeds.org/April_03/htm.

9. John Gottman, *The Marriage Clinic* (New York: Norton, 1999), 41–50.

10. Gottman, 41–50.

11. Kaja Perina, "Covenant Marriage: A New Marital Contract," *Psychology Today* (March 1, 2002), http://www.keepmedia.com:/Register.do?oliID=225covenantmarriagehtml.

12. Harville Hendrix, *Keeping the Love You Find: A Guide for Singles* (New York: Pocket Books, 1992), 247.

About the Authors

DRS. BEVERLY AND TOM RODGERS have been Christian relationship counselors for the past twenty-six years. They own and operate Rodgers Christian Counseling and the Institute for Soul Healing Love in Charlotte, North Carolina. Both have a PhD in Clinical Christian Counseling. Bev's master's degree is in marital and family therapy, and Tom's is in human development.

They have appeared on the television shows *A Time for Hope*, *His Side Her Side*, *The American Family*, and *NBC Nightside* and have been featured speakers on NPR and the BBC. Together they facilitate relationship workshops for couples and singles across the globe. They have been married for thirty years and have two grown daughters.

If you want to learn more about the Institute for Soul Healing Love, please contact Bev and Tom at (704) 364-9176 or visit them at www.SoulHealingLove.com.

GRAB HOLD OF THE LIFE YOU CRAVE.

5 Paths to the Love of Your Life

Winner, Chediak, Holland, Wilson, Clark, and Lindvall
1-57683-709-2

Respected relationship experts help you gain new insight into dating and marriage. Try out their advice, see what works and doesn't work, and discover your own personalized path to the love of your life.

Every Thought Captive

Jerusha Clark
1-57683-868-4

Jerusha Clark examines the sources of our insecurities, unholy desires, and anxieties. Drawing from her own experiences, Clark shares insights from God's Word that provide a road map to victory over toxic beliefs.

Visit your local Christian bookstore, call NavPress
at 1-800-366-7788, or log on to www.navpress.com.
To locate a Christian bookstore near you, call 1-800-991-7747.

NAVPRESS
BRINGING TRUTH TO LIFE
www.navpress.com